Caring for People

A workbook for care workers

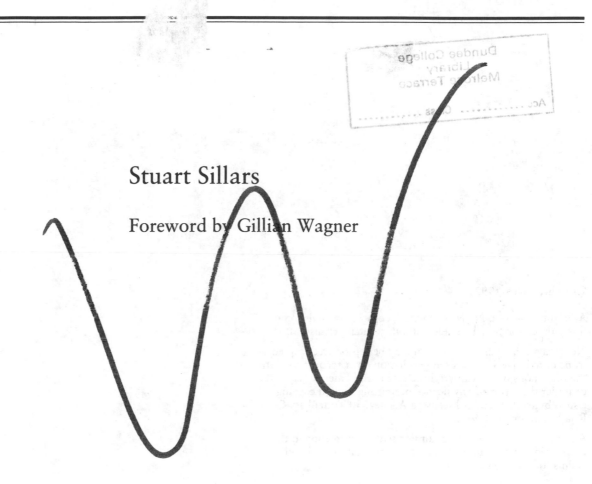

Stuart Sillars

Foreword by Gillian Wagner

MACMILLAN

For Lynda King
and the staff and residents of
Rose Cottage, Broughton

First published 1992 by
THE MACMILLAN PRESS LTD
Houndmills, Basingstoke, Hampshire RG21 2XS
and London
Companies and representatives
throughout the world

ISBN 0-333-57054-5

A catalogue record for this book is available
from the British Library

Filmset by Wearset, Boldon, Tyne and Wear
Printed in Great Britain by
UNWIN BROTHERS LIMITED
The Gresham Press, Old Woking, Surrey
A Member of the Martins Printing Group

10 9 8 7 6 5 4 3 2 1
01 00 99 98 97 96 95 94 93 92

Contents

Foreword

This is a book whose modest title belies its importance both for those who are care workers and for those in need of care. It does not replace training, but should help to give confidence to care workers starting out on their careers and also to the people they care for. Its aim is to give care workers a broad introduction to the practicalities of caring. It does this in simple, clear language and provides an admirably straightforward system to enable care workers to check for themselves that they have understood the multiple tasks that they are called on to perform in the course of their duties.

It would surprise me if the book did not also provide an incentive to keep management on its toes, as care workers are frequently (and rightly) encouraged to talk to their supervisors about subjects ranging from policy for confidential information in the care setting to the establishment's policy for dealing with aggression or procedures to be followed when people leave care.

There are several reasons why I welcome the publication of *Caring for People*. Firstly, I do not know of another publication which sets out so clearly and explicitly the many aspects of a care worker's duties. Some of the procedures may seem routine and a matter of common sense, but common sense cannot be taken for granted. More importantly, the cumulative effect of reading through the variety and range of skills required of a care worker as set out in this workbook helps to reinforce the fact that caring for people is a very skilled, complex and professional job. Whether readers are looking after someone at home, learning informally, or working towards a qualification, they will find the way in which the book is set out stimulating, interesting and helpful.

Secondly, the whole ethos of *Caring for People* is very much in line with *A Positive Choice* (the Wagner Report) which stressed that the client's needs should be at the centre of provision in residential care. This is well illustrated by the author, who writes: 'What you're doing is immensely important – helping people to endure trying circumstances with dignity and as much independence as they can, and helping them as far as possible to enjoy life.'

Finally, I welcome the fact that this book covers the complete range of care in a seamless whole. This, I think, is important because the underlying philosophy of care, the objective of which is to provide the best quality of life for those who have lost a degree of independence, is the same whether you work in a home for older people; are assisting a carer to care; or helping to prepare someone for independent living. I hope that all who use this book will find it both an enriching and an enjoyable experience.

Gillian Wagner

Acknowledgements

Many people have given generously of their time and expertise during the preparation of this book. I should like to thank the following for their help: Lynda King, Proprietor, Rose Cottage Residential Home, Broughton, Cambridgeshire; Emma Lee, Community Support Worker (Mental Health), Westminster Social Services Department; Michael Key, Day Services Manager, Derbyshire County Council Social Services Department; Valerie Farebrother, Director, Division of Community and Academic Studies, West Kent College; Jan Kermeen, Hospital/Community Liaison, Community Unit, Huntingdon Health Authority; Terry Smyth, Head of Community and Educational Studies, Colchester Institute; and Chris Cook, Training Consultant.

The National Vocational Qualification statements on p. 107 are reproduced by kind permission of HMSO. Photographs are reproduced by kind permission of Arjo Mecanaids Ltd. (p. 62); J. Allan Cash (p. 102); Ebony of Mayfair (p. 64); Macmillan Press (pp. 99, 102); Medical Support Systems Ltd. (p. 68); MENCAP (pp. 48, 51); National Association of Citizens' Advice Bureaux (p. 80); NCH (pp. 25, 31); Remploy (p. 49). The remaining photographs were taken especially for this book by Peter Hayman, whose tact and professionalism I acknowledge with pleasure and thanks. Anne Webster of the Macmillan Press provided much support and encouragement during the writing process; Andrew Nash edited the text with accuracy and sensitivity.

Despite this wealth of assistance, any errors and omissions which remain are of course the result of my own perversity; but, here as nowhere else, I hope that words have not failed me.

Stuart Sillars
March, Cambridgeshire

1 Getting started

This chapter is designed to introduce you to the business of caring – its demands, its rewards, its language, and some of the key issues it involves. It also describes what this book aims to do and suggests how you can use it to increase your knowledge and skills, whatever your circumstances. You might, for example, be:

- learning informally;
- working towards a National Vocational Qualification (NVQ) or Scottish Vocational Qualification (SVQ) to help with your job;
- studying at college or on day-release for a BTEC, City & Guilds or other award in caring;
- looking after a friend or relative at home.

Whatever your circumstances, the book is designed to give practical help and guidance. *Caring for Older People: creative approaches to good practice* by Terry Smyth (Macmillan) is a related book which deals in more detail with the care of older people in residential, domiciliary and day-care settings.

The next section discusses some key terms used in care, and some key principles. Activities designed to make you more aware of these principles follow.

Then come two longer sections on fundamental elements of care – people's rights, and how to plan and give care. As well as giving you essential information, these sections will help you get used to the kind of learning process you'll go through in the rest of the book.

A word of caution: this isn't a book in a conventional sense – it's more a self-study text which you need to work through slowly and carefully. Some parts will take you a few moments to work through; others will take an hour or two. The activity on page 105 is designed to help you to plan your learning. A little care here is worthwhile as it can save problems later on. However you use this book, make sure that you work through these opening pages to begin your training as a care worker.

1.1 Who cares?

If you're just starting as a care worker – either with a job or at a work placement in a course of study – you might well feel that you're setting out on something alarmingly new. But when you think about it, it will be similar to many things you've done before. Looking after people is one of the oldest human activities; it's something that we all do at least some of the time.

There are many ways in which you might already have been carrying out some of the essential duties of a care worker. You might, for example, have had to look after younger brothers or sisters, perhaps helping to wash or feed them, or taking them shopping and seeing that they're safe. Perhaps you have looked after a parent or guardian when he or she was ill. If you share your life with another person, there will have been times when caring and nurturing are part of the relationship. And if you're a father or mother, you'll be familiar with care at all levels, from changing nappies to being there when needed to discuss emotional problems; from building confidence in times of stress, like the first day at a new school, to knowing when to stand back and let the young adult make his or her own decisions – even if to you these seem wrong!

On top of this there are skills that are too often taken for granted but that are really high-level management skills which most of us need to make sure that our lives run smoothly. These might include knowing, when you're unwell, whether to take an aspirin or call an ambulance; organising a schedule of tasks at work, at home or in your studies; or sharing responsibilities with a partner or family member.

Running a home demands complex skills which are often not given due acknowledgement. Many a company director, cushioned by a secretary or assistant, would find it impossible to work at such a pace and in so many different roles.

Your previous experience gives you a strong basis to build on – caring is something you're already used to doing. This book aims to help you develop the skills you have already, and to acquire new ones to become an efficient and professional care worker.

1.2 What this book does

This book is designed to help you gain the knowledge and skills you need to be a professional care worker.

It gives you advice on the topics you need to know about to contribute fully to care, whatever the setting you work in.

It also gives questions, activities and projects for you to check that you have understood the ideas and can relate them to the care setting in which you work.

Learning with support

Although you'll be working through the book and doing many of the activities yourself, you won't be working alone. You'll find that many of the activities ask you to talk something over with your supervisor or to work with a care-worker colleague.

As the appendix (page 105) will show, you'll also need to talk with your supervisor to plan exactly which parts of the book you need to use, and the order in which you'll tackle them.

So it's really a team effort – like so much else in caring, you'll get more out of it and do better if you see yourself as one of a team working together.

Learning in a context

Throughout the book you'll be encouraged to relate what's being said to the care setting where you work. That's very important. After all, what matters is how well you care for people, not how well you know what's in this book or any other. So try always to bring these two things together:

- the ideas of the book;
- the real situation of your care setting.

Using this book

You'll probably find that not all of the sections of this book are related to the care setting in which you are working. *How* you use the book depends on *why* you're using it. This might be:

- to help you find your feet when you start as a care worker, with the help of your supervisor or employer;
- as part of a training programme run by a college or health authority;
- to prepare for an NVQ/SVQ award in care;
- to prepare for a BTEC, City & Guilds or other first-level award in care.

To get the best from it, you need to work out:

- which sections you're going to cover;
- how long you're going to take over it;
- what help you're going to need.

In the appendix at the end of this book, you'll find an activity designed to help you plan your learning by sorting out which parts of this book are relevant to your needs, and making a timetable to help you work through them.

Working at it

Whichever sections of the book you use, remember that they're designed to be worked at, not just read. As you look through them you'll find:

- questions with spaces for you to write the answers;

- activities which get you to find out information – from your supervisor, from care specialists and from other sources;
- activities which ask you to play the role of someone you care for, to see how this person might feel;
- longer projects on collecting information or studying your clients so you can help satisfy their needs.

All of these are things to do, not to take for granted. They'll get you involved in the business of care, by:

- making you think about situations;
- getting you to experience a little of what your client experiences;
- making you find out about local services and facilities.

Even if you think the answers are obvious, or the activities take too long, please do them. Get into the habit of answering the questions and doing the activities right from the start. They'll all help to build your understanding and involvement in caring.

Quick reference

Another way to use the book is as a source of information and help on particular subjects. The index lists topics and areas of care so that you can find what you need quickly: the contents list (pages iii and iv) gives a more general guide to what's discussed where.

Keeping it going

Caring is a cumulative process. You don't stop doing one task just because you've covered it in a book and have gone on to the next.

Think of each section as a building brick: it's separate at first, but when you've taken it and made it part of your study it's an essential part of a larger structure of care.

If you're working for an NVQ/SVQ award, you'll need to show evidence of the skills you've gained over a period. And, of course, these skills are basic to the business of caring – so you'll need to keep using them all the time once you've covered them in your programme of learning.

Your own notes

While working through this book, keep a file for your own notes. These might include:

- names of people whom you can contact for specialist help;
- special techniques and approaches to particular problems;
- kinds of apparatus to use for specific situations;
- places where you can obtain special equipment or supplies.

What this book *doesn't* do

This book isn't a medical encyclopaedia. It doesn't give detailed guidance on specific techniques of care. It doesn't tell you how your own care setting should be run. All of these are issues which you need to get more specialist help on – from a doctor, or from your supervisor or employer.

Instead of this, it aims to give you a broad introduction to the practicalities of caring, which will be most effective when it is used in conjunction with help from your care setting, your colleagues – and, of course, the people you care for.

1.3 Key words

Some of the words used in this book have particular meanings which are rather different from those they have in general use. The most important terms are discussed below.

Carer

Although in general conversation this means anyone who cares for someone else, in this book it is used to refer to someone who cares for a friend or relative, usually looking after her in her own home, or visiting her on a frequent and regular basis.

Often there is no difference in practice between what a carer of this kind does and the work of a professional; but, because very often someone who is employed in caring has to help and support family carers, it's important to use different words to make clear who is who.

Care worker

This is used to mean someone who is professionally employed in the day-to-day care of people. It doesn't include specialist members of the care team, like nurses, physiotherapists, occupational therapists or social workers: these people are referred to by their more specific names.

Supervisor

This refers to the person who will be most directly in charge of your work and your learning as a carer. He or she could be:

- a social services manager in a day centre;
- your employer in a residential home;
- a staff nurse in a hospital where you work as a health care assistant;
- an officer-in-charge at a residential home for children;
- a tutor in a college;
- another care worker who is guiding you in your training.

Whoever it is, this is the person who will be guiding your work as a care worker and your learning while you are going through this book.

The person who actually supervises your work and learning may not be the person whom *you* usually call your supervisor – the title is given to different roles in different situations. Your supervisor at work *may* also supervise your learning, but not necessarily. And if you're doing the work-experience part of a college course, your college *tutor* will be your supervisor – but he or she will work very closely with the person who's supervising your work.

Care setting

The place where you do your caring – the residential home, day-care centre, or the house or flat where the people you are caring for live independently.

Care agency

The body which employs you as a carer. It could be a local social services department, a hospital, a private residential home, or any other organisation which provides care.

Care team

The group of people involved in looking after a client. It will involve some or all of the following.

- doctors;
- nurses – including specialists like psychiatric nurses;
- specialist therapists – physiotherapists, speech therapists, occupational therapists, and perhaps art or drama therapists;
- chiropodists;
- continence advisors;
- managers, supervisors or officers in charge of residential or day-care centres;
- voluntary workers.

It's important to get to know your care team early on – you'll find activities on this later in the book.

Client

Professional carers use the word 'client' to refer to a person they care for. To the outsider, this word can appear formal, distant and the very opposite of what you'd expect from people who care. It seems to suggest someone who buys life insurance or double glazing rather than a person who needs help.

In a sense, that is one reason why it's used. It suggests a *professional* relationship with the person being looked after, rather than one based on sentiment. It also encourages a professional distance, to prevent your becoming too involved emotionally with the people you're looking after.

Your own care setting may not use this word to describe the people it cares for. Some common alternatives are:

- 'resident' – used for someone who lives in a care setting such as an old people's home;
- 'day patient' – someone who attends a daily programme in a hospital;
- 'user' or 'member' – someone who uses a day centre.

In this book, I've sometimes used 'clients' and sometimes 'people', because it seems important to stress that, while you're being a professional, the 'clients' you're dealing with are people with feelings.

You may have your own ideas about the word 'client' and the relationship it suggests between the carers and the cared-for. If you're happy with 'client', that's fine. If you aren't, think about what word you'd use instead. It's an important issue, since it goes to the heart of your role as a care worker. Think about it and talk it over with your supervisor and other care workers. You may not reach a satisfactory conclusion, but talking about it will help you consider more carefully what you're doing and what you hope to achieve.

A word on gender

The English language today isn't very good on words which cover both genders. The old idea that 'he' covers both male and female has quite rightly been rejected; but if you use 'he or she' you then have to use 'himself or herself' and sentences get long and awkward. The form 's/he' isn't much better – how do you pronounce an oblique stroke?

Throughout the book I've used 'he' or 'she' alternately when referring to clients or other people – mainly for simplicity but also to show that people being cared for are, of course, of either gender. Whenever 'he' is used, it should be understood to mean 'he or she'; wherever 'she' is used, it means 'she or he'.

There is no assumption that particular roles, jobs and attitudes are the preserve of one gender – whichever our sex, we can all be equally responsible, equally distressed, equally vulnerable.

1.4 The larger setting

Caring for people doesn't take place in a vacuum. The practical side is essential, of course – but there are larger issues on which it rests. To understand the implications of a lot of the things you do, it's important to know something about the theory behind care. This falls into two areas: legal and ethical.

Legal considerations

In the 1980s a series of reports and White Papers emerged, leading to various Acts of Parliament which have changed considerably the way in which care is organised.

The *Griffiths Report* of 1988 stressed the need for co-operation between all agencies involved in caring – local authorities, health authorities and individual care settings. A White Paper called *Caring for People* suggested dividing care organisation into care agencies – that is, local authorities who pay for care – and care providers – that is, residential homes, day-care centres and other bodies who actually do the caring. Care should be centred, it said, on what the client needs, decided by an assessment by care professionals. *A Positive Choice* (the Wagner Report) of 1988 stressed that the client's needs should be at the centre of provision in residential care.

Two recent Acts are important. The National Health Service and Community Care Act 1990 incorporates the provisions of earlier reports; and the Children Act 1989, which was implemented in October 1991, places the needs and rights of the child at the centre of provision in cases of child care, divorce and similar matters.

Care settings are also affected by other, more general laws. The Food Safety Act 1990, various Food Hygiene Regulations, the Health and Safety at Work Acts, the Fire Precautions Act 1971, and the Data Protection Act 1984 all control ways in which care providers organise and carry out their duties.

> **ACTIVITY**
>
> With your work supervisor, discuss ways in which items of legislation have a bearing on how care is carried out. You don't need to know every Act in detail, but you do need to know how each affects the setting in which you work.

Ethical matters

These are concerned with the moral rights and wrongs of care. Should an elderly person live on her own, even when at risk of accident or malnutrition? Should a child who is mentally handicapped go out on his own?

Questions like these frequently have no clear answer: the arguments on both sides are strong. You may or may not have to take ethical decisions in your life as a carer – but even if you don't, you need to be aware of the existence of the debate about ethics and the fact that very often the answers are far from straightforward.

1.5 Being a professional

Being professional as a care worker means two things:

* having a fund of knowledge and skill to draw on in your work;
* keeping your own feelings under control when dealing with people you care for.

The first is relatively straightforward – this book will help you acquire the knowledge and skills you need. The second, though, can be difficult. Working with older people, seriously ill children or people with severe mental handicaps can be upsetting and exhausting. To cope with it, you need to find a way of keeping your feelings at arm's length.

If you don't, you may form emotional attachments which could be harmful to you. They could also get in the way of caring. Some things – helping people to be independent, telling them for their own safety what they can't do, taking control in emergencies – will demand clear thinking of the sort you can't have if you're feeling distressed or 'sympathetic'. So learn to put such feelings to one side so that you can concentrate on caring in a professional, efficient way: knowing what you're doing, why you're doing it and how it will benefit the person you're helping.

It's not as simple as that, of course – you *will* get emotionally involved, and will have to find ways of dealing with that emotion. When someone you're caring for is ill, or dies, or moves away, there will be feelings to sort out.

You need to be aware of this, and think how it's going to affect you. There are no easy answers here, but the best approach is being able to talk about the situation, express your feelings, and move on to whatever comes next. Your supervisor, employer, or other people you work with are important here. Talk to them about your feelings when things get difficult. Even if talking is upsetting and draining, it's better than keeping feelings bottled up: this can lead to clinical problems like depression and anxiety. More experienced colleagues will have had the same reactions to the business of caring; they'll be able to help you cope.

Finally . . .

Being a care worker can be exhausting, both physically and emotionally. Often you'll work long hours for little reward. People outside the care setting won't understand what you do. There may be no answer to some of the problems you have to deal with. The people you care for may be unkind and unpleasant to you. Their relatives may criticise your approach.

But there is another side. You'll be with people in periods of great suffering, and develop very close bonds with them. You'll get to know as individuals the people you care for, and there will be many rewarding friendships as well as times of sadness and loss. Often, the people you care for will help you get through the times of sadness, as well as the other way round.

However important someone may be, there may come a time when he or she will need care of an intimate and basic kind. Remembering that will help you understand what it's like for the people you care for – it's something that any of us might need at any moment.

What you're doing is immensely important – helping people to endure trying circumstances with dignity and as much independence as they can, and helping them as far as possible to enjoy life.

1.6 Key principles

Whatever the setting in which you care, and whatever the nature of the people you care for, there are some key principles which will always be important. This section helps to make you more aware of them by giving you some activities to complete. This will also introduce you to the way the rest of the book works. For both these reasons, you should set aside some time so that you can carry them out thoughtfully and thoroughly.

Respecting the individual

People are people, whether or not they are being cared for. You need to respect their individuality and their privacy at all times.

ACTIVITY

1 Choose a person you know well, but who is an independent adult. If possible, choose a family member – husband, wife, brother, sister.

Look at these caring tasks:

1 Doing shopping.
2 Making financial arrangements (e.g. paying large bills with the person's money).
3 Discussing the client's medical condition with her doctor.
4 Helping her to dress.
5 Cleaning her teeth.
6 Taking her to the lavatory.

Imagine that you have to perform these tasks for the person named. After careful thought, write down:

(a) What would the person feel about having this done for them?
(b) Under what circumstances would you do it for the person?
(c) How would you make it easier for the person?

2 When you've done this, choose another person who is very different from the first. Try to select someone who is:

- of a different gender;
- of a different temperament;
- much younger or much older;
- of a different ethnic background.

Comments

What you have found out from this activity will be quite revealing. And difficult, of course: helping people in very intimate ways isn't something that's ever straightforward. From the exercise, you may have learnt many things, but two will probably have been the strongest:

1 helping effectively without being too intrusive of people's rights to privacy is something that needs great care and thought;

2 as people are individuals, the right way to help will differ with each person.

These are vital principles: remember them and apply them.

Ethnic groups

People from different ethnic groups have different cultural traditions and beliefs; we all see things from our own viewpoints.

Test your own knowledge of the range of cultural beliefs by answering the questions below.

1 Which group celebrates Chanaka and Yom Kippur?
2 Members of what religion eat only fish on Friday?

3   How would you help a Hindu woman to dress or undress?
4   What are Muslim teachings about contraception?
5   What arrangements for washing are necessary for Sikhs?
6   Whom would you contact to give comfort to a Sikh who is dying?
7   By which of a Muslim's names would you address him or her?
8   What is the Catholic church's teaching on abortion?
9   If a member of the Anglican church asked to receive communion, whom would you contact?

Some of these points relate to beliefs, some to practical matters; most are concerned with both. You need to be sure that you know about the religious or cultural background and beliefs of people you care for, so that practical details of care can be arranged according to their preferences. It's really an extension of matching care to the individual.

There may well be times when the practical demands of caring conflict with the religious and cultural beliefs of an individual. Often there will be no easy or obvious solution, and you'll have to discuss things with the person involved, her relatives or religious leaders, and your supervisor. But being aware of the issues is a major step towards finding a solution.

Do all you can to explore the beliefs and customs of those you care for. Do this by talking to them, and to other members of their community, and by reading widely on the subject. You'll find useful books listed under 'Further reading' at the end of this book.

Communicating

Whatever you do as a carer will be influenced by communication. To begin with, there's the matter of words. Even if you speak the same language as a client, there may be words that mean different things to the two of you, or words that he knows and you don't, or vice versa. Sometimes a client won't speak English – you may need an interpreter who speaks Gujarati or Demotic Greek.

But communicating isn't just a matter of words. It is also influenced by gesture, facial expression, what you wear, and where you are when you talk with the other person. Several sections of this book discuss this in more detail; for the moment, it's important that you realise just how essential communicating is as a way of giving support and building trust, as well as giving and receiving information.

ACTIVITY

1 Choose *six* people. Try to cover as wide a range as possible in terms of:

(a) age;
(b) gender;
(c) background;
(d) attitudes;
(e) how well you know them.

2 Look at the following situations in which you would need to communicate with these people:

1   asking whether they need to use the lavatory and whether they need help;
2   reassuring them when they've had a fall, are in pain and you're waiting for medical help;
3   persuading them to eat some lunch;
4   telling them arrangements about moving to a new care setting.

Write down how you would communicate with each of the six people, matching what you say and how you say it to their own natures:

(a) kind of language;
(b) facial expression;
(c) gesture or touch;
(d) how you'd encourage them to respond.

3 Now think about how you'd communicate with someone who

(a) is deaf;
(b) is blind or visually impaired;
(c) can hear but not speak.

If this has left you feeling that communicating is quite impossible, then don't worry – the activity is meant to be difficult. But then communicating is hard, too. Words are fragile things, and we all use them in subtly different ways.

Developing the skill of communicating is something we all need to work at, all the time. Like the other key issues in this section, it isn't something to be kept separate. Knowing about the difficulty is the first step forward – keep thinking about it and you'll find ways of getting through to the people you care for.

The care team

Whatever your situation, you're not alone in giving care. You're a member of a team. Your supervisor will have details of the other members. As well as specialist therapists and social workers, they'll include local religious and community leaders.

In your work file, write down the names of the people you'll be working with. Next to their names, write down their work address and telephone number. Make a point of getting to know them as soon as you can, so that when you need their help you'll know those with whom you're working.

1.7 Individuals and rights

The people you care for have the same needs, desires and rights as the rest of us. This is something you need to remember all the time. Especially if you work in a residential care setting, you need to do all you can to avoid people becoming 'institutionalised' – losing their independence and the freedom they would have if they lived alone.

You also need to fight against treating all clients like children – 'infantilisation', as it's sometimes called. Treating everyone in the same way, assuming that they cannot make the simplest decisions, giving them help with basic tasks that they can well perform themselves – these are all approaches you must guard against.

In practical terms there are two key areas to this: the need to keep the client's individuality; and the need to respect his or her rights.

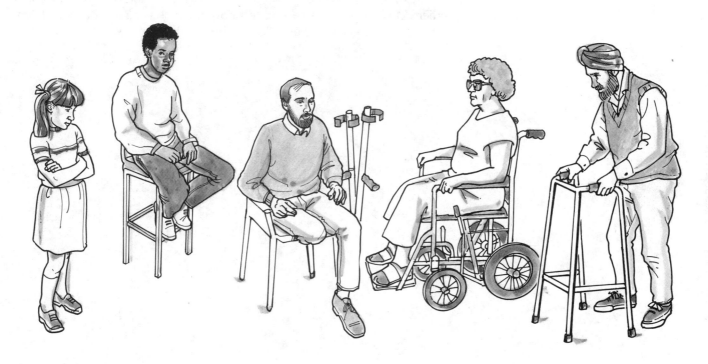

Keeping a personality

Being cared for involves losing individuality and privacy in a lot of ways. You may have to do without important possessions; you'll miss people you used to have around all the time; and your daily routine will be decided by someone else. These are things that, as a care worker, you need to keep remembering.

All of this can lead to a loss of any sense of personal worth. Older people will see themselves excluded from activities they once enjoyed; younger ones will see others growing up and gaining freedoms they can't share. As a care worker, one of your most important jobs is to see that people continue to value themselves in these circumstances.

Make a start by being sure that you're calling the person by the name she prefers. As soon as possible after you first meet someone new, ask what she wants to be called, and check that you're pronouncing it correctly. Use the person's name, too – simply saying 'Hello, Mrs Ruddock' as you walk past in the morning can show that you value as an individual each person you care for.

Make time to talk and listen to the person, too. This is something covered in section 2.4, but it isn't something you can separate from other aspects of caring. Finding out what a person thinks, listening carefully to what he says and taking it seriously are fundamental to every aspect of caring. You need to invest time in talking with people, to build a relationship of trust. Make sure, too, that any aids to communicating are made available: hearing aids, voice boxes and other devices can all be of immense value for some people in maintaining human contact.

While you're talking, guide the client towards the positive things about her situation: 'It's good to have memories to look back on', rather than 'It's sad that it's all gone now'; 'Your wheelchair lets you do pretty smart turns in basketball', not 'Your wheelchair means you can't shoot so high'.

Although you should always encourage, there'll be times when you need to tell a client that he isn't behaving appropriately. If someone's always asking you for help he doesn't need, or if someone makes endless complaints, you should make clear that what he's doing isn't right in the circumstances – but, again, do so by suggesting a more positive alternative. Often this will be in the form of friendly advice about how to respond to a particular situation.

Sometimes, too, you'll have to talk to a client about acceptable and unacceptable sexual behaviour. It's a difficult subject; section 2.11 looks at it in more detail.

ACTIVITY

1 Work with a colleague, preferably someone you don't know well. He or she will take on the role of a care worker in your institution; you will take the role of someone just coming in to be cared for.

Respond to the questions you are asked by your colleague as part of the usual admission procedure for your care setting. All the time, think about how this makes you feel. Does it help you feel an individual? Does it stress positive things? Were you given time to answer? Did the care worker listen?

2 When you've finished, swap roles. While you're talking to the 'new client', remember how you felt in that role. Do all you can to make him or her feel valued and important.

3 Afterwards, ask your colleague how effective the process was, and discuss ways in which you could improve your ability to make the client feel valued.

Beliefs and practices

Respect for the individual includes respect for his beliefs. It's not enough to assume that all old people like to sing hymns and tune in to *Songs of Praise* each week. Though that may be enjoyed by some, it won't be appropriate to everyone's beliefs.

It's important, first of all, that you find out about people's beliefs. Your setting may have a procedure for this – if so, follow it carefully and make sure that records are written accurately and legibly.

Whatever your clients' beliefs are, make sure that you take them seriously. You may not know the difference between a Sikh and a Muslim, but that shouldn't stop you from accepting the value and importance of such creeds to people who hold them. Find out what services or facilities are available locally for the various beliefs your clients have; make contacts with their leaders, and invite them into the care setting.

This relates to practical things, too. Diet, clothing, festivals – all of these are relevant here. Very specific points can also arise. If a dying man asks his bed to be turned to face the east, don't object because it causes problems for the cleaners: this is a practical expression of a deep religious need, and it is essential that you take it seriously and comply with it if at all possible.

ACTIVITY

1 Talk to some of the people you care for about their beliefs. Ask them whether they have the opportunity to express them fully. Make notes, and pass them on to your supervisor for inclusion in the clients' files.

2 Find out about the religious centres in your local community. Make contact with their leaders, and see whether arrangements can be made for people you care for to go to services, or for leaders to visit your care setting.

Rights to choose

Being cared for doesn't mean losing the ability to do anything for yourself. Still being able to do things – eat, walk, make the bed, make the tea – is important for many reasons. At a physical level it makes sure that the body gets exercise; at a mental level it keeps thinking processes alive; and at an emotional level it provides interest and – even if in small doses – some sort of stimulation and a sense of self-esteem. The satisfaction gained from not feeling completely useless and dependent is worth a very great deal to us all. It's essential, then, that you do all you can to encourage people you care for to do things for themselves – as other sections of this book will keep stressing.

One aspect of this is getting the client to express preferences and make choices. This can apply to many small things – diet, clothing, what newspaper to read – but also to larger matters. The National Health Service and Community Care Act 1990 makes this quite explicit, and many care settings now have a written policy of involving the clients in such matters.

Involvement means explaining various approaches clearly and in suitable language, and listening sympathetically to the client's response. It may mean helping her to express ideas – but not prompting or putting words into her mouth.

Whether or not you can follow the client's wishes is something the care team as a whole will need to decide, often on the basis of medical advice. This is another area where working as a team is vital.

If problems arise over a client's preferences, tell your supervisor. Arrive at decisions by discussing issues with appropriate people – the client's relatives as well as other professionals – while maintaining confidentiality.

If you think the client is not being given a reasonable choice, or his wishes are being denied, then again you need to talk to your supervisor: it won't be easy, but the client must come first.

ACTIVITY

1 Talk to your supervisor about the procedures in your care setting for giving choice to your clients. Include day-to-day matters such as diet and meal-times, but also larger ones such as forming care plans.

2 Talk to your clients, too. Ask them if they have enough freedom of choice and, if not, what improvements could be made. Then discuss things again with your supervisor.

Exercising rights

All the above has pointed to one thing: clients are equal partners in their care, not passive receivers. This is important in another key area, too: the rights of people who are being cared for. Rights are of two kinds: social and legal.

Social rights

These are the rights we all expect to enjoy in any setting involving other people. They include:

- privacy;
- dignity;
- the right to choose diet, dress and occupation;
- the right to choose whom we see and associate with;
- the right to be alone;
- having a say in the way that the care setting is organised.

Many care settings have had a clients' charter or other document which sets out the rights of people being cared for, and with the coming of the NHS and Community Care Act this has become a legal necessity.

If you think these rights are being abused, it's your duty to do something – by tackling the person involved or by talking to your supervisor, perhaps.

ACTIVITY

1 Think about the basic rights you consider important for yourself. They may relate to privacy, freedom of beliefs, or practical things like being able to listen to the radio when you want to. Make a list of your ideal rights.

2 Choose one or two of your clients. Discuss these rights with them and ask how they would change them. After a while you'll have a list of rights.

3 Compare this with any charter or statement of rights that your care setting may have. If necessary, suggest changes or improvements to your supervisor.

Legal rights

These rights exist to ensure that someone in care has the same protection from the law as anyone else, and are stressed in recent community-care legislation. They include:

- freedom from physical or mental abuse;
- protection of the individual's property;
- protection of the individual's finances.

Legal rights do not cause problems for clients who can look after their own affairs and possessions. They can, however, pose problems for those who cannot manage their own affairs through age, illness or other circumstances. There may be issues of finance or ownership to be discussed, and important decisions may have to be taken about a client's future or possessions. In all cases, try to encourage and support the client to decide independently but with appropriate advice. Get the client's friends or relatives involved and, if necessary, get professional help from a lawyer or social worker: the local Citizens' Advice Bureau (CAB) will probably be able to help here.

The essence here is again communicating. Do all you can to help the client to communicate, by using appropriate aids where necessary but also by being prepared to listen. If you do this, the client will feel that the decision, however difficult, has been arrived at after careful and thorough consideration, and that she has not given up her rights.

If you're caring for children or young people, the position about rights may be governed by legal circumstances. Nevertheless, the same essential points apply. Listen to the person's own preferences and reasons and do all you can to meet them – or to explain why they can't be met. Children have very few formal rights: do all you can to respect those that they have, such as privacy, and show respect for their views and feelings. The Children Act 1989 has made the position a little clearer, but in many areas this still has to be applied in practice.

ACTIVITY

1 With your supervisor, form a clients' support group for the people you care for. Arrange to have regular meetings to discuss issues related to clients' rights such as those raised here.

2 Invite along clients' relatives, or perhaps a solicitor or other specialist from your local CAB. Remember, though, that this should be a forum for the clients – your role is going to be largely that of a listener, taking note of what's said and trying to put into practice what the clients want from their care setting.

1.8 Planning and giving care

Caring doesn't only involve the obvious things, like helping with food, dressing and mobility. These things are vital, or course, but they only make sense when they are seen as part of an overall care plan, which sets out the client's needs and how they are to be met.

Most care institutions now work on the principle of a care plan for each client. Helping to draw up such a plan will help you to understand the reasons for what you are doing, and thus give you a better sense of purpose in your caring activities.

Planning care

The first task is to discuss the nature of care required by each client. Each care setting will have its own procedure for this: in some you will simply be told what to do, whereas in others you will be involved in discussions with other professionals.

However the plan is arrived at, you need to have a very clear idea of the nature of the plan and of your role within it. If you are unclear about these, either at the outset or when you begin to implement the plan, ask the advice of your supervisor. The same is true of your larger position in the care team: the exact nature and limits of your responsibilities is something you need to know about, so be sure to ask if you are in doubt.

You may also need to explain to others their roles in the care plan, especially if there is confusion or overlap in tasks. If this happens, or if the process of care seems to be at risk, you need to talk to colleagues to sort things out. Should you think of ways to improve the care plan, these too should be conveyed to your supervisor as soon as possible.

The key to a successful care plan is that each person involved should know what he is expected to do, and how this contributes to the overall aims of the care. If you're ever uncertain, ask; if, you think things can be improved, talk to other care workers. And, of course, details of the care plan should be discussed only with people who are qualified to know – other care professionals, the client, and the client's friends or relatives.

ACTIVITY

Talk with your supervisor about how care plans are formed in your care setting. In particular, discuss:

(a) the written format they take;
(b) the procedures for drawing them up;
(c) the procedures for reviewing them;
(d) the division of responsibilities in care;
(e) who has the right to see the care plan.

ACTIVITY

Talk to other care workers and other members of the care team. Find out:

- their special areas of responsibility;
- areas where their roles touch or overlap with yours;
- what information they need from you to help in their caring;
- what information they can give you to help in your work.

Organising care

If you're going to care effectively, you need to know exactly what your responsibilities and duties are. This is something which your supervisor will usually make clear – but it's important that, if you're in any doubt at all, you ask.

This applies to practical things as well as other aspects of care. Knowing which tasks take priority when you're on duty, and who does what when you're working with a colleague, are aspects of your work which you must sort out clearly and quickly.

From time to time you'll need to take on new duties – dealing with a new aspect of care, using new equipment or working in a new setting. When this happens, you need to be sure of yourself if the client is to feel comfortable and trust your judgement – so make sure that you get proper advice or training before you start. As far as possible, try to get experience of as many different kinds of care as are offered by your centre. This will improve your versatility and value as a care worker, and will also add to your self-confidence in dealing with all kinds of situations that might arise.

Teamwork

Essential to successful care is the ability to work as part of a team. Getting on well with clients is vital, of course; but don't let it overshadow the need to get on with the people you work with. Knowing who does what in practical terms is often the basis of this, but it goes further. A relationship of trust between all members of the care team is essential, so do all you can to develop this.

Trust can be developed in practical ways. Always pass on information quickly and clearly – if you can't finish a job, or need help in an emergency, for instance, say so. Similarly, listen to colleagues and help them whenever you can. If you have any ideas to save time, increase efficiency or improve care standards, talk them over with the care team.

Encourage health

It's easy to assume that people's health can't be improved or changed when they are being cared for – particularly for long periods. Do all you can to encourage clients to improve their own condition. This doesn't mean raising unreal expectations: rather it means getting people to be realistic about what they can and can't do, but to push the limits of their health as far as they can and live in a way that's as stimulating and fulfilling as possible.

Talk to them in an appropriate way about their health, offering them advice and, if necessary, showing them aids like diet charts, diagrams and other materials. Clearly the ways of improving health need to be both realistic and appropriate, but they might include points such as suggesting they take more exercise, or eat more fresh fruit. Involve your clients in the discussion by encouraging questions, and get specialist help from other members of the team if necessary. All of this will not only help the clients' health: it will encourage them to think positively and take part in their own care, in itself a valuable outcome.

Your own behaviour when caring will clearly be an essential part of the care plan. What you actually *do* is vital here, but so are related things like how you dress, talk and move. Being part of a professional team means that you should perhaps be more formal than when talking to personal friends – but it doesn't mean being arrogant or distant.

Once again, it comes down to knowing your part in the care plan and being able to contribute to it. This means:

● caring for clients according to the plan;
● asking for advice and information when you need them;
● helping other care professionals when necessary;
● following the overall aims of your care setting.

ACTIVITY

1 Talk to a client about his health. Discuss how he feels, and how he'd like to feel. Together, work out some realistic aims for improving health.

2 Now think about which other members of the care team you need to consult for advice. Bring them into the discussion.

3 When you think you've found ways of improving the client's health, raise them the next time the care team meets together – or suggest them as changes to the care plan next time you see your supervisor.

If you've worked right through this section, you'll see that it has gone round in a circle – from finding your role within a care plan to suggesting ways of improving that plan. That's how it should be. A care plan isn't something that's fixed and static – it's something that changes and develops with the changing needs of the client and the care team. Working with the team and the client, and having the trust of everyone involved as you extend your own care skills, will ensure that you contribute fully to this constant development of care, both in planning it and in carrying it out.

2 Supporting and communicating

This chapter deals with the different ways and different situations in which you will need to help your clients. It covers topics such as:

- getting, giving and keeping information;
- communicating with clients;
- helping clients to communicate with you and with others;
- developing relationships with clients;
- helping clients in particular situations of different kinds.

Although each separate section deals with a particular area of caring and the skills it demands, there are some themes and issues which run through the whole of the chapter.

Communication

Communication lies at the heart of the business of caring. For down-to-earth practical reasons, you need to be able to get through to clients – to tell them where to put their feet and hands when you're helping to move them, for example.

You also need to encourage them to communicate with you – to tell you if they are in pain or discomfort, to say what they would like for breakfast, and a great range of practical, everyday matters.

Communication has a larger function, though. As you develop the ability to communicate with someone, and to help her communicate with you, you develop a relationship based on trust. Caring depends on a good many factors and skills, but trust is one that is fundamental to them all. Unless the client trusts you, she won't communicate, essential treatment or medication may not be given, resentment may develop, and the client's health – physical and psychological – may get worse.

Supporting

Supporting is the business of just being there to encourage and reassure someone. It's something that many of us do all the time without knowing – for friends, children, spouses or family members.

Supporting can mean different things in different settings. It can mean being prepared to listen to someone's woes; it can mean encouraging someone that he *can* walk to the bathroom if he wants to; it can mean reassuring him when something has gone wrong.

Whatever form it takes, it depends a great deal on mutual trust – and fundamental to that is the ability to communicate, both by listening and by talking.

Relationships

Everything mentioned so far depends on building a relationship. Most obviously this will happen with the people you care for; but others are involved too.

There will be other members of the care team, whom you'll need to ask for advice, and whom you'll need to help at times, during treatment or in recreational or other activities.

There will also be the friends and relatives who visit your clients. They will need support, too, and you'll certainly need to develop a relationship of trust here, so that they feel confident in the way you and your care agency are looking after the person they are close to.

Relationships between clients matter a great deal. If you have clients who are young adults, you'll need to be aware of their developing sexual and emotional needs. This means being aware of practical issues, but also showing sensitivity towards people's emotions – we don't stop feeling just because we're being cared for, remember.

The social unit

Although we talk impersonally about 'the care setting' or 'care agencies', people in care are really part of a community – a social unit like a family, place of work or any other organism where people work and often live together. This is something you need to be aware of, and which many of the sections will discuss in more depth.

Knowing that you're part of a community which cares but which is not fussy or intrusive can be a source of pleasure, support and nurture to people in care – so you should always try to develop this social side of your work.

Information and confidentiality

Keeping information up to date is a major theme of this section. In an emergency you may need to have a client's details ready at a moment's notice, so knowing where they're kept is essential.

You may also need to keep records or write reports on clients or events. These will range from a note of fluid intake for someone who is unwell to writing a report on a distressing incident involving two clients. Whatever it is, it should be done:

- quickly – before you have time to forget;
- legibly;
- in the manner followed by your care setting.

A related issue is confidentiality. Who has the right to know details about a client? This is something on which your setting will have a clear policy which you need to know about.

Privacy

Although the care setting is a social unit, remember that your clients are individuals. They need their privacy, too. Keeping a balance between privacy and social contact isn't always easy – but just being aware of the difficulty, and respecting your clients' dignity as individuals, will go a long way towards getting it right.

In general

The last few paragraphs have looked at a series of themes as if they were separate issues. But, of course, they're not. Communication, trust, confidentiality, relationships, support – they're all part of a single framework which is really the basis of a great deal of human experience, let alone of caring.

An awareness of the close links will help you to develop better relationships with your clients, and become involved in the social community you're part of, without losing the professional skills and insights that you'll need to be effective as a care worker.

2.1 Collecting and giving information

Imagine that, one morning, you discover someone lying on the ground with a deep cut on the head, apparently unconscious. Medical help is needed fast. But for it to be successful, the doctors probably need to know vital information – allergies to drugs, possible causes of the fall, and any number of other details which can only be gained from the client's confidential medical records.

Filing may not be the most exciting task, but it can be vitally important. Unless records are kept up to date and in proper sequence, information which may be vital will be delayed.

Not all information will be as important as that, of course – as well as keeping records for the use of dietitians, therapists and other professionals, you need to keep them for other people. Other care workers will need to be informed of any changes in the condition or behaviour of clients, in a day book or whatever other system your setting uses. Social services staff will have to be told of a client's state at home, and the kind of special support she needs. Anxious relatives will want to know how their son or mother is getting on; and the clients themselves will want to know about their conditions.

So storing, retrieving and giving information is a central part of the job of the care worker. It's not only something of practical importance, either: you need to be aware of ethical issues too. Who has the right to see confidential information? And what of the client's rights? These are all topics covered in this section.

Storing and using information

Every care setting will have its own way of storing information, whether a filing cabinet or a computer. When you need to get hold of information, make sure you know how to do so – check with your supervisor about this. When you've taken the information from its store, make a note that you've done so, in the record book or file record provided. That way, no one will waste time looking for something that's not there.

In some settings, information will be kept in a different way. A common procedure is for each care worker to be responsible for information concerning a small group of clients. This will be kept by you – perhaps in a separate drawer of a filing cabinet. This will take away some of the need for checking and recording information when you remove it; but it puts a greater responsibility on you to make sure that it's kept in order and can be retrieved quickly when necessary.

However it's kept, information must be used properly once it has been retrieved from storage. This could mean:

- checking that the person who requested it has the right to see it (even in the most open systems, permission will be needed for a client to see medical records);
- passing the written records to the person who requested it;
- getting people to sign for documents as a record of where the documents now are;
- telling someone verbally what they wanted to know.

If you need to pass information to another member of the care team, or a social worker, make sure you know how to do this – is there an internal mail service, for example? Or should you drop it in at the local health centre or social services office? However it's done, make sure *all* the necessary information is sent, and that it's accurate: this is especially important in verbal messages.

Sometimes you'll need to add information. You may need to ask another care worker for some detail: if so, enter it into the records as soon as you can. If necessary, get your colleague to sign the information to show who has provided it. Write records accurately and legibly – there's no point in writing a note that no one can read.

When you've used the information, make sure it goes back in exactly the right place. If it's confidential, mark it 'confidential' or use whatever system your centre has to keep things private. And finally, if you think there's anything wrong with the filing system, tell your supervisor.

Who needs to know

Confidentiality is always a sensitive issue. You could argue that the more people who know about a client's problem, the more there are to help with it. But what about privacy? People being cared for need it just as much as the rest of us.

Often it's a matter of deciding how much information should be given. For example, if a client is to be rehoused, you'll need to tell the housing authorities about her physical condition to help her get a ground-floor flat. But do you need to disclose that she has been diagnosed HIV-positive?

There are legal considerations too. The Data Protection Act 1984 makes organisations register the fact that they keep information about others on a computer system: unless you're registered, you shouldn't keep such data on computer files.

Then there are the needs of the clients. If someone asks for more information, make time to talk to them – find out what they want to know and, if necessary, get help on whether or not to tell them. Make sure you have a clear idea of what it is they want to know, too – talk carefully to establish this. When you know what's needed, check with your supervisor and, if the agency's policy agrees, tell them.

Usually these issues are decided by someone in authority. But you need to know who. If you're in any doubt, ask your supervisor before giving out information. If you don't do this, you could cause problems for yourself and the care team – and a lot of distress for the client.

> **ACTIVITY**
>
> Talk to your supervisor about the policy for confidential information in your care setting. Summarise it in a couple of sentences in your work file.

Telling it

Talking to clients about themselves needs care, understanding, and a lot of time. Sections 2.2 and 2.3 suggest ways in which you can communicate to build trust, and you'll need to use all of them when discussing items of information which may be difficult.

The first thing is to check that you've selected the right information. You may have to say who you are before you start, to avoid confusion: 'Hello, I'm Sara: d'you remember you asked me to find out about . . . ?' Then talk to the client in words she will understand – though don't patronise. Take things slowly – break it down into a simple, stage-by-stage approach.

Sometimes you might need to show the client drawings or documents – a diagram of the body for a child, perhaps, or a note from a doctor or social worker to reassure someone who is convinced he's not being told the truth. From time to time, check that he understands what you've said. And above all, be reassuring and encouraging.

At the end of the talk, make sure you've told the client what she wanted to know – or, at any rate, as much as you can. Afterwards, think about the consequences of what you've said: is the person going to behave differently, perhaps because she knows about her medical state, or that a social worker will be calling? Consequences need thought – so be prepared for what might happen next.

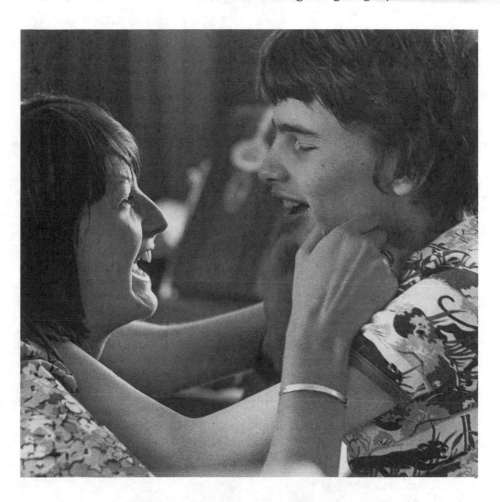

ACTIVITY

1 Watch an experienced colleague telling a client some important information. Notice the language used, how he or she stands or sits, and how he or she checks that the client has understood.

2 Now, with the help of your supervisor, try talking to another client in the same way to convey information. Afterwards, talk to your supervisor about how effectively you did it.

It's not only clients who need to know things. Doctors, therapists, social workers, housing officers, staff at benefit offices – all these and other professionals may need information. How much information you give them will depend on the situation: if you're in any doubt, ask your supervisor.

Friends and relatives will want to know how the client is, or perhaps practical details like the length of stay in care, or what kind of help can be given in the client's home. There are two rules here:

1 if you're not sure whether the person should be told something, check the confidentiality rules of your setting;
2 if you don't know, say so and refer the person to someone who does.

ACTIVITY

1 Write a checklist for giving information to a client. Begin with the given items and add others of your own.

(a) Am I sure this is the information he or she wants?
(b) Does she or he know who I am?

2 When you've finished, check your list with the points made in the last section.

Information on the phone

Very often people will ring for information. They could be other care workers, relatives, or social services staff.

First, be careful about confidentiality. Follow your centre's usual rules about giving information: if you don't know who they are, or are unsure, then don't give them confidential information. Ask them to ring back, and meanwhile get advice from your supervisor.

Get to know the mechanics of answering the phone. Answer politely and say where and who you are – 'Good morning, Belmont Day Centre, Rajkumar Sharmi speaking.' If you can give information, do so quickly; if not, say so. Sometimes you'll be able to transfer the call. If you can, tell the caller what's happening, and explain things to the person who's taking over.

If you can't help and there's no one else available, take a message: get the caller's name, number and – if you're unsure – his relationship with the client. Then ask what the message is. Write it legibly, and pass it on straightaway – or leave it somewhere where you know it will be seen by your supervisor.

Talking on the phone isn't always easy – a connection may be bad, or the caller may have noise in the background. Speak clearly, and check that you've been understood. Repeat things if necessary, or be prepared to call back at a more convenient time.

Remember, too, that people calling for information may be upset. Be patient, and try to help as much as you can – but remember, too, that you need to get back to your clients as soon as you can. Don't be afraid to be assertive and bring the call to a polite but firm close if you think you're getting nowhere, or if you are being drawn into giving information without proper cause.

ACTIVITY

1 Ask a colleague to call you and make an enquiry about a client in the role of someone who has no right to the information. Practise taking the call – first of all answering clearly and suitably, then explaining to the caller why you can't give the information.

2 Afterwards, discuss how the approach might have been improved. Repeat the exercise until you're confident in answering the phone, taking messages, and giving – or refusing – information.

However hard we try to communicate well, there are times when we misunderstand each other. You're discussing issues which may be of great importance to the people you care for: so be patient and try to understand their concern.

2.2 Making relationships work

Getting on with clients

THINK...

Think for a moment and then write down:

(a) how important it is to get on well with people you care for;
(b) why.

Some answers:

(a) Vital – it's as simple as that.
(b) Lots of reasons:
- you have to give simple instructions and understand what they tell you – failure to do this can cause unhappiness or harm;
- knowing that you're friendly and understanding will help the client to trust you – and that's vital where personal care is concerned;
- being close to people can improve clients' psychological health – they feel better because they feel valued and understood;
- being close is important to all of us – and when you're ill or need care, it's even more so;
- you'll spend a lot of time with each other: it's more pleasant if you get on.

Getting on well with clients is vital, then: but what does that actually *mean*? Some things are fairly straightforward – the kind of thing you do naturally, like greeting people in a friendly way when you see them, and being there to talk when needed. As every other section in this book stresses, you need to talk to your clients to explain what's going on – when helping them to move or dress, for example.

But you won't always be free to chat – so be firm when you must move on to something or someone else. It's also important to set limits – to make

clear that you can't give all your time to one person. If a client keeps calling you, or ringing an alarm bell for no reason, or asking for help when he doesn't need it, you need to be firm. Explain that other clients have needs, and that you can't give all your time to one person.

ACTIVITY

1 In your work file, write down three or four phrases you can use to bring a conversation with a client to an end in a friendly way.

2 Now think of how you would explain to a client that he or she shouldn't keep calling for help when it's not needed.

3 When you've written your own versions, discuss them with other care workers or your supervisor to decide what the best approaches are. But remember: there's no single right answer, as every client is an individual.

Sometimes, you'll need to *help* the client to communicate. You'll find more on this in section 2.4.

Getting on with visitors

It isn't only clients you need to get on with – there will be relatives and visitors too. They may need careful handling – they'll be upset and worried, distressed or perhaps feeling guilty that they aren't doing the caring themselves. So how do you get on with them? The activity on the right will help.

You might have included simple things like smiling and greeting them – by name, if possible. Or practical things like offering tea or coffee. Getting them involved will build trust, too – ask them if they'd like to give Dad his tea, or hold Indira while you take her pulse. But, again, practices vary: some care settings will ask relatives to leave during examinations, and you should find out and follow the setting's practice in this.

But be careful – some people will take naturally to this but others will find it difficult. Do all you can to avoid giving the impression of disapproving – relatives can feel miserable and guilty enough at the best of times, and a misplaced comment or unfriendly grimace can cause a lot of upset.

ACTIVITY

Make a list of ways in which you can establish and build relationships with clients' relatives and friends.

Larger issues

There are other points which you need to think about when communicating with relatives and visitors.

Confidentiality is essential. There are four rules:

1 *don't* talk about clients if they can hear you – unless you're consulting another care professional and the client is involved in the talk;

2 *don't* talk where others can overhear confidential information;

3 *do* make sure the person you're talking to has a right to know – asking who she is can be done pleasantly and easily if you do it when you first see her;

4 *do* follow the practice of your care institution about giving information – if you don't know what this is, find out and summarise it in your work file.

Getting on with other care workers

As well as clients and their visitor, you need to get on with other care workers. Be prepared to work at this. Talking to clients can be tiring and difficult, and lead to all kinds of frustrations, so tension can build up: make sure it isn't released by arguing with other staff members.

ACTIVITY

1 For each of your clients, make a list of visitors with whom you can discuss the client's condition.

2 Now make a list of places in your care setting where you can talk privately with them.

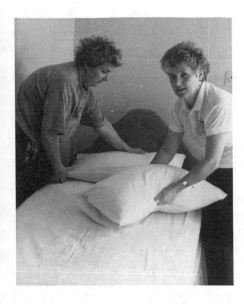

> **ACTIVITY**
>
> In your work file, list two situations where you need to get on with other staff members for practical reasons.

There are some very important ones:

1 telling others important information quickly;
2 getting help from supervisors or specialists;
3 getting help from colleagues.

If you know the other people you work with and you all trust each other, you can do these things better – so work hard at getting on.

There are other things you can do to build trust. For example, if you respond to someone else's request for help quickly and efficiently, they'll help you when you need it.

> **ACTIVITY**
>
> Write down other practical ways to build trust.

Here are some ideas to compare with yours:

- Only ask for help when you really need it.
- Try to share tasks equally – it's unfair if one person gets all the tough jobs.
- Arrange to swap duties if someone has an important date.

A lot of this comes down to getting on with your supervisor in sharing the organisation and running of the care institution. Here are some ideas for longer-term projects:

1 Co-operate in drawing up schedules of work – cleaning, caring, tea-making – so that everyone gets an equal share.
2 Work out a way in which suggestions for improvements can be discussed by all the care workers.
3 Think about ways in which work rotas and timetables can be spread out to help all the care workers.

When it fails . . .

We're all human. There will be times when you can't bear the sight of someone, or when you think no one ever listens. When that happens, talk about it – to your supervisor, or to a colleague who can do something about it; not to a family member who can offer sympathy but not a solution. Of course, there will be times when you have to talk to someone close; it'll help release frustration. But don't do it all the time: you won't get professional advice, and you'll put extra strain on the relationship.

Talk to your supervisor about how you can resolve problems in working relationships. You might find it helps to have a clear procedure for this, or you might prefer to keep it informal. But remember that it will probably happen – talking about it can only help.

2.3 Supporting clients and their relatives

People who are being cared for need a lot of support. They may feel apprehensive or anxious about what is going to happen to them; they may feel lonely; and they may feel unsure about their own physical or mental states.

To a smaller extent, the same is true of their relatives. They may be unused to being in a care setting, and will feel powerless about what is to happen to someone they are close to, and perhaps feel guilty that there is not more they can do themselves.

As a care worker, a major part of your role will be to help and support both groups.

Making people welcome

Do all you can to put people at their ease from the first moment that you meet them. You need first to establish who they are, and encourage them to feel at home. This is especially important when you're admitting a client.

When you've put everyone at their ease, you may need to direct friends or relatives to a waiting room while you look after the client, or tell your supervisor so that appropriate arrangements are made. If there is any delay, keep people informed; in this way they will remain relaxed, which will help any admission or other procedures to be got through as smoothly as possible.

As well as making people feel welcome, you may have practical things to attend to when admitting clients. Visiting times, arrangements for cash and valuables, and other arrangements will have to be made clear. You may need to check medical or other records for the client, and tell your supervisor about anything that seems incomplete or unusual. Finally, if you need to fill in any forms or complete any records about admission, do this as soon as you can, making sure that they are accurate and legible.

As well as admitting clients, you will probably have to welcome people who come to visit them. You'll need first to find out who they are. If necessary, ask them to wait while you find out whether they can see the client – there may be a restriction on visitors, or it may not be a convenient time. Be polite, but be firm: most people will understand that there are rules or procedures to follow.

When you're talking to people, whether they are clients or visitors, try to match your language and behaviour to theirs. That way you'll be sure of being understood. Section 2.4 has more to say on this, and on how to keep trying when you think you're not getting through to someone. Watch, too, for signs of unusual behaviour, especially distress in clients – that way you'll be more prepared to help deal with any upsets if and when they occur (see section 2.6).

ACTIVITY

Talk to your supervisor about procedures for admitting a client. Find out:

- where clients are admitted and where visitors can wait;
- what procedures must be completed;
- who has responsibility for medical records;
- what forms, if any, must be completed;
- who usually looks after admissions;
- what rules or procedures there are about valuables and possessions.

ACTIVITY

1 With another care worker – preferably someone you don't know well – go through the approach you would follow when welcoming a visitor. Make him welcome, but be firm about checking whether he can see the client. If you can, get a third person to observe.

2 Afterwards, ask the 'visitor' how well you did.

Did you make him feel welcome? Did you seem officious? Get comments from the observer, too – how did it seem to her?

3 Repeat the exercise, changing roles, until you feel confident that you can carry out such an exchange in practice.

Finding their bearings . . .

When they arrive, clients are going to be confused and perhaps a little afraid. Help them to settle in by showing them where everything is and introducing them both to other people being cared for and to other staff members. Make a particular point of showing them bathrooms and lavatories – many people are embarrassed about asking where these are.

A little later, talk with them about how your care setting works. Mention things like meal times, daily or weekly events, and arrangements for special care needs. Point out emergency aid buttons or other practical aids. Don't overwhelm, though: take it gently, going at the person's own pace. Encourage the new client to ask questions and, in the first week or so, make a point of seeing whether she knows where everything is and is settling in comfortably.

Above all, try to avoid anything which is going to cause distress. Be caring, but not fussy: build a relationship of trust so that she feels at home with you, and you with her.

ACTIVITY

1 Talk to someone who has been in your care setting for a little while. Ask him about what happened when he came in. What was he told? What was left out? What would have made settling in easier?

2 When you've finished, talk to another care worker or your supervisor about what he said. Make a few notes about things to do to help new clients feel at ease – and put them into practice next time someone new comes along.

Helping friends and relatives

If your client has regular visits from friends or relatives, you'll probably get to know them quite well. Even if you don't see them often, though, make them welcome by greeting them in a friendly way. If circumstances permit, let them see the person they've come to visit in private; if this isn't possible, try to explain why.

Sometimes it helps to get visitors involved with the care plan. Tasks like giving a client food and drink, or even more routine tasks such as arranging flowers, can make a visitor feel wanted and remove a sense of embarrassment by actually having something to do.

Try to build a relationship of trust. Explain to visitors the facilities your care setting can offer. Use language which is clear and straightforward but not patronising. Be as honest as you can with them about a client's condition, treatment or other aspect of care; if you can't answer a question yourself, say so – and say who can. If there's anything you can't explain, or if the visitors want to know more, tell your supervisor or get advice.

ACTIVITY

1 Talk to your supervisor about your clients and their regular visitors. Choose one or two clients and for each one:

- list the regular visitors;
- make a note of their relationship with the client;
- find out what they should or should not be told

about the client's condition, where some information is confidential.

2 When you see these people, make a point of introducing yourself to them. Then work to build the relationship of trust discussed in this section.

Keeping in touch

People in care often find it hard to keep up relationships with friends and visitors whom they don't see often. In some cases – if they have memory disorders, for example – it can be hard for them to remember who these people are. So they need help to maintain contacts that can be important links with the outside world and the interests they used to have – an essential consideration if and when they return to life outside the world of care.

Do all you can to encourage contacts. If the client can make contact himself, make sure he has the facilities – take him to a payphone, for example, or encourage him to write. Talk about things which interest him, to try to keep alive the link with friends between visits.

If a client can't write or telephone, perhaps you could offer to write for her, following her wishes – and writing legibly so that her friends can read it. Similarly, if a letter arrives, make an occasion of it. You may need to read it aloud to her – in private, so that others don't overhear.

Confidentiality is also important when talking about your clients. Make sure that, if you need to tell a visitor something about someone in your care, you do so in private – and, of course, don't disclose such details to people who aren't relatives or close family friends of the client.

When a visit is arranged, help the client to prepare – perhaps by encouraging her to wear something special, or think of things to talk about.

Remember that because you're with the client a good deal of the time, you may end up being told all sorts of things about the client's family: 'My sister never liked me', 'My son doesn't care' – all the things that distressed and lonely people feel and often say. If this happens, accept that the feeling is real to the speaker, but don't let it colour your response to the visitors.

> **ACTIVITY**
>
> *1* Make a list of ways in which you can help a client to keep links with friends or relatives he doesn't see often.
>
> *2* Talk to another care worker about this, and make a list of ways you think would help.

Making moves

There will be times when clients leave your care setting, to go back to their home or to another care centre. How to help in the process of the move itself, the transfer of records and other practical points are discussed in section 2.8. As well as these, though, you need to consider the effects of such a move on friends and relatives.

If the client can arrange the move, fine; do all you can to encourage self-reliance, especially if a client is going back home. If the client can't make the arrangements, try to get the friends or relatives to help – and if they could be there for the move, their support would help a great deal.

Take the client to the point of departure with the friends, encouraging and reassuring as much as you can. See it as a new beginning, even if you're sad to see the client go.

> **ACTIVITY**
>
> *1* Talk to your supervisor about people leaving care. Make sure you understand any special procedures and approaches your care centre may have.
>
> *2* Next time someone leaves your care setting, try to go along and see what happens. Think about how things could have been changed – if at all – to make friends, relatives and the client more involved with the process. Put these thoughts into practice the next time someone leaves.

2.4 Helping people to communicate

Getting through

Communicating isn't just a matter of getting through to other people: they have to get through to you, too. And if they're ill, old, unhappy or disabled, they may need help – both in grasping your message, and in responding. But unless you can get your point across, you won't get anything in return.

THINK...

Write a caption for each of these pictures. The captions should stress important practices to follow when talking to clients.

Important approaches include:

- Making sure your client can see and hear – check that spectacles or hearing aid are being worn if needed.
- Communicating at face level and keeping eye contact while you talk.
- Talking at a suitable volume, and matching your tone and expression to the client's.

Of course, *what* you communicate is important too. It's no use talking about something you know the client isn't interested in. And it's no good using language he isn't used to – and that could mean very simple words as well as difficult ones. Do what you do when talking to anyone else: try to match the subject and the expression to what they know and are used to. And always encourage; look friendly but not patronising, look for any sign that the client has understood you, and nod and smile to respond to this.

Remember that clients are just like the rest of us – individuals, with our own likes and dislikes. Make sure you look at the care plan for each client (see section 1.8) before you begin communicating – though after a while you'll get to know each person's specific needs.

ACTIVITY

Think about some clients you have in your care. Write a few lines saying which is the best way to communicate with each – what kinds of words, tone of voice, special equipment and other techniques you need to use. If necessary, consult the care plan.

What if I can't get through?

There will be times when it seems as if you just can't make contact with a client. When this happens, ask yourself:

- *Can I be seen?*
- *Can I be heard?*
- *Am I using the right language?* This doesn't only mean using words the client would use. It also means using an interpreter who can speak Punjabi or Gujarati, or whatever the client's language is. In practice your supervisor will be responsible for obtaining interpreters – but it's an issue you need to be aware of.
- *Am I using the right body language?* Standing with crossed arms can look very aggressive; kneeling or squatting at eye-level is much closer and more friendly.

ACTIVITY

What do you do if that fails? Think about this and then write a couple of suggestions in your work file.

Here are some possibilities:

- try taking the client's hand or arm;
- try writing a message for the client to read;
- try showing a photograph or drawing a picture.

What if it fails?

If you try everything you can think of to get through to the client you'll usually succeed in some way; but there will be times when you won't.

When this happens *ask* for advice. And don't worry: outside the care setting we all get on with some people better than with others, and occasionally fail even with our closest friends. Getting help is the best approach when all else has failed and you really need to make contact.

Listening

Sometimes a client will want to get through to you in reply to a question. At other times, she will want to communicate for another reason – to express hunger, pain, or other bodily needs, or to seek comfort and reassurance. So it's vitally important that you're aware of this.

Look carefully, listen carefully, and try to help the client to self-expression.

THINK ...

Look at the illustration on page 33, and discuss the ways in which the carer is helping the client to communicate.

When you've asked a question, encourage the client to respond. That *doesn't* mean jumping in with a prompt, or another question. It means listening and showing that you're listening – and waiting a good long time, if necessary, for the client to reply. Sometimes it will be difficult – but resist the temptation to nag or hassle the client, which will only make things worse. Be especially patient if the client has a speech impediment. Jumping in and saying what you think the client is trying to say won't really help.

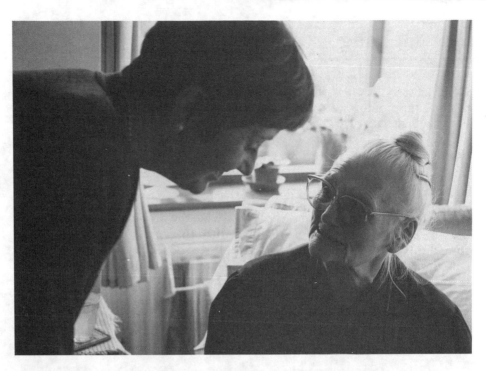

Listen with your eyes, too: the slightest nod or blink could be a way of communicating, with a stroke patient, for example, or someone very distressed.

ACTIVITY

1 Look at your institution's care plans or records and make notes in your work file about how each of your clients communicates. Add to it from your own experience, too.

2 Discuss this with other carers and use it to help you understand your clients' responses.

When you do get a response, show that you've understood. Nod, smile, talk, squeeze the client's hand – all of these show that human contact has been made. Contact of this sort is important when anyone communicates: when you're ill, confused or unhappy, it's essential.

Finally: remember that in many cases you're the client's lifeline and source of human contact. Communicating well, and helping him to communicate, will not only make him feel wanted and valued: at times it will help relieve pain and distress too.

2.5 Helping to comfort

Comfort is both physical and emotional. A lot of it may have to do with plumping up pillows, or making sure the temperature of the room is right; but it will also involve keeping distress to a minimum, both for the client and for any others involved. So what may look like fairly routine activities become rather more important when seen in this light.

Keeping discomfort down

You can only help someone if you know what the problem is, so the basis of making people comfortable is helping them to express themselves. This is something that's covered in section 2.4 – it depends on a great deal of encouragement from you, using suitable language and building trust so that the person feels able to tell you how she feels.

You'll also need to know what you can and can't do to help the client. This means talking to the care team – to find out about how the client should sit or lie, for example. It also means talking to the client before you start moving him, using suitable language or, if necessary, an interpreter.

ACTIVITY

Talk to your supervisor about the clients you look after. For each one, try to assemble a brief set of notes on:

- whether they become distressed;
- what causes distress;
- how it can be helped.

This will probably take some time, especially if you have several clients. But make a start with those who are most often distressed. As well as giving you more knowledge of the people you care for, knowing what to do will give you confidence when you need to deal with someone in distress.

If you feel you can't help, you need to tell your supervisor or get help. You may need to monitor someone's condition too – make sure records are kept promptly and legibly in the approved manner for your care setting.

If you can help, do so gently. Always explain what you're doing while you're doing it – 'I'm just smoothing your sheets, Mr Jones' – and, if necessary, tell your supervisor what you've done.

You may also need to help other people. If someone's been calling out, for example, other clients need to be reassured that everything's under control. Do this quickly and efficiently – be sympathetic, but make clear that you're in control of the situation.

Physical matters

Helping the client to be comfortable and feel rested is the main priority here. Move slowly and quietly, and do all you can to reassure the client. But there are other things to consider.

THINK . . .

In your work file, write down other factors which are important in the client's comfort.

There are several. You might have said:

- people nearby should move quietly and with consideration;
- heating, ventilation and light should be as the person wants them;

Distress is often shown in people's postures – look out for signs like these

- faults or disturbing elements should be put right or removed – a dripping tap, someone vacuuming, traffic noise;
- prescribed drugs should be given in accordance with the doctor's instructions.

All of these are essential if the client is to feel comfortable and rested. Of course, if there's something you can't put right, you should tell your supervisor as quickly as you can – but often a very slight change can have very good results.

Remember to keep an eye on the client. This may mean leaving the door of her room ajar so that you can see her as you walk past; or it may mean checking at regular intervals. The care plan should make clear what to watch for: monitor the client and report any changes as soon as you can. Watch for practical problems, too: if you can't put them right, tell someone who can.

Preventing distress

People being cared for can often feel distress over what might seem very small things – changes to routine, dark weather, and events in the news which would be unimportant for most of us. It's essential that you take these as real feelings, and don't just brush them away thoughtlessly.

As always, be gentle and reassuring, using language, tone of voice and body language that are suited to the person and the situation. Often just making clear that you know that the client is upset will help him a lot – and it will also increase trust and confidence, of course.

Other matters are important. If a client's belongings have been re-arranged, or are not as she wants them, this can cause great distress: if *you* had only a few photographs in a shared room, *you'd* be upset if they were moved, too.

People who are upset can't always talk easily about their worries. You need to give them time. Make sure the setting is right, too – distress is made worse in public, so help the client to a private place if it's at all possible, or close the door if you're in the client's room.

There will be times when all your efforts to comfort the client achieve little. When this happens – or when you're not sure how to go about it – you'll need to get advice. This might be from your supervisor, or it might be from another care – a community psychiatric nurse, say, or another specialist member of the care team.

When things are calmer, think about what happened. What caused the distress? What did you do to help? What did others do? Make sure that you record these facts and circumstances: as well as forming an important part of the client's record, they will make things easier next time – for both of you.

ACTIVITY

1 Work in pairs. One of you should take the role of a client who is distressed but cannot explain why, and try to communicate this by mood, gesture and sound (not by continuous speech). The other should seek to comfort – by speech, touch, tone of voice and any other means you can think of.

2 Afterwards, the 'client' should talk to the 'care worker' about how effective his or her comforting was, and how it might have been improved.

3 Now change roles and repeat the exercise.

Afterwards, use the experience you've gained when trying to comfort people who are distressed. It will also help when trying to communicate with people whose first language is not English and when there is no interpreter available. Remember, though, that people are individuals: what worked in one case may not work in another.

2.6 Dealing with disruption and aggression

At times, you will find yourself caring for people who can be disruptive. This may take the form of arguing with care workers or with other people who are being cared for – what's often called 'verbal assault'. It may spill over into physical aggression.

Dealing with this is not easy, and often there are no obvious answers. This is a very specialised area of study, and you'll need to get advice from specialists in the care team – a doctor or a community psychiatric nurse, perhaps. But there are certain approaches which you can take to minimise risk and discomfort to yourself, the other people involved and the person who is causing the disruption.

Preventing disruption

The best way to deal with aggressive or disruptive behaviour is to prevent it from happening. This means finding out two things:

- what causes it;
- how it can be avoided.

To do this, you need the help and support of other members of the care team. If someone is known to be aggressive, you'll probably have a case conference to sort out all the facts, sharing information and pooling suggestions on how to defuse potentially risky situations.

Getting to know the signs of disruption before it occurs is a key skill which specialists can help you with. There may be physical signs, like shaking, uneven speech, or changes in complexion and breathing; or certain people may respond unhappily to certain places or situations.

Deciding what is and what isn't acceptable is something else the care team will have to decide. What's the difference between raising your voice and shouting? When does reaching out become striking out? Talk about these things so that, when they occur, you'll be better able to react suitably.

Sort out, too, what action you can take in response to people who are disruptive. Isolation in their own room is probably the most likely, although such matters must be approached with extreme care and caution. Talk with your supervisor to sort out what actions – often referred to as 'sanctions' – can be taken in your care setting, and under whose authority.

Above all, do whatever you can to avoid triggering aggression yourself; and keep everyone else in the care team informed of anything you see which suggests either aggression or success in avoiding it.

Dealing with aggression

However good you are at preventing aggression from starting, there will probably be times when it erupts.

If you're involved when an aggressive episode takes place, the vital thing is to keep a cool head. Respond as a care professional, not as a person: this will help you to remain detached. You need to be *aware* of your own feelings, though, as repressing them can have unhappy consequences for you. Talking over how you felt, with another care worker or your supervisor, soon after the incident can help you to get through and learn from difficult times like these.

When you come across aggression, the first step is to assess rapidly what's going on. You need to consider:

- what's actually happened;
- what might happen;
- the danger to others;

- the danger to yourself;
- the cause.

Weigh these up carefully. If you think you can deal with things yourself, do so; but if there's any doubt, get help. Do this by pulling an emergency help cord, if there is one, or by sending someone to get another care worker or your supervisor. Unless there's no possible alternative, don't get other clients involved in helping: it's unfair to ask them, and may cause barriers between them and the aggressive person which will make the latter feel even more isolated.

ACTIVITY

1 Study the illustration and imagine that you've just come into the room to see this happening. Assess the dangers of the situation and make decisions about:

- whether to call for help – and how to do so;
- what to do about the cause;
- how to treat the aggressor;
- how to minimise risk.

2 Afterwards, talk to other care workers about how *they* would approach the situation.

What you actually do will depend on the situation, and your centre's policy for dealing with aggression. Whatever it is, remember to protect others who are nearby, and to protect yourself. Damage to property is regrettable, of course; but far less so than damage to people – and people, especially people in care, are fragile.

Be positive, but be tactful in your response. You need to strike a balance between taking things seriously enough to take control, and not being confrontational and so making them worse. This *doesn't* mean that you should not be assertive: often a confrontation will be necessary. It *does* mean thinking carefully about whether this would be the best approach in the circumstances. Don't patronise the aggressor; this will inflame things further. Everything you do should be aimed at *reducing* tension, not increasing it. As far as possible, try to remove the cause of the aggression, if there is an external one.

There are various techniques for dealing with aggression. 'Matching and leading' depends on carefully observing the level of aggression in the person's speech and body language; then matching it in your own behaviour; and then gradually becoming calmer, in the hope that the aggressor will follow you back to normality. It may work – but it can also make things worse, so get professional advice about using it.

Another technique depends on getting your eyes at the same level as the aggressor's. If it's a child or young person, kneel or sit to be on their level: this removes the idea of authority at once, and can often be very successful.

Physical restraint is the very last resort. Aim to control but not harm; secure the aggressor on his or her back on the ground, by shoulders, wrists and knees – but *only* do this if you've been taught restraint techniques, and you're certain that no injury can result to anyone involved.

You may need to administer first aid – section 2.7 discusses this. But make sure that the aggression has been calmed first, or that you are quite clear who is doing the calming and who is giving the first aid – otherwise, things will only get worse.

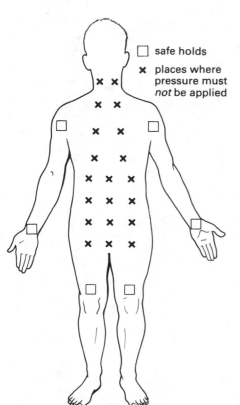

☐ safe holds

✗ places where pressure must *not* be applied

Techniques of restraint

ACTIVITY

1 Arrange a time to talk to your supervisor about your care centre's policy in dealing with aggression. In particular, ask for advice on specific techniques such as matching and leading, and approaching physical restraint.

2 If necessary, ask the advice of a care specialist, and act out situations so that you know how you should react in a real situation.

Afterwards

When it's over, give people time to calm down. Separating the aggressor from anyone else involved may help – but do it tactfully and with care to avoid further flare-ups. A little while later, discuss things – separately – with the aggressor, and with the others. Encourage them to talk, to express their feelings; it may take time, sometimes a few days, for feelings to emerge, but for the sake of all concerned it's important that they do come out.

As soon after the incident as possible, write a report or fill in a report form. Use this as the basis of a discussion with the care team. The team will need to decide how to avoid such things happening again, so it's essential that you report the incident accurately, while it's still fresh in your mind.

Aggressive incidents are disturbing and upsetting things: it's natural that you yourself will be upset after one has occurred. Talk about it to a colleague. As well as letting you express your feelings, this will help you to get advice, or work out other ways of dealing with the situation. And although your sympathies will probably be with the innocent parties involved, remember the aggressor: it's often those who are least likeable who need the most help.

2.7 Dealing with emergencies

However well run a care setting may be, there are bound to be some occasions when things don't go to plan. No two emergencies are ever the same – different people will be involved, different problems will have occurred, and different actions will be necessary to resolve them. And in many cases it won't be that there is just one right answer or one ideal course of action.

But emergencies can be prepared for. By having a clear set of procedures to follow, and an ordered list of priorities, you can do your best to sort things out and get help to those who need it quickly and efficiently.

This section looks at the more common emergencies and suggests how you should tackle them. It doesn't talk in detail about techniques of first aid, or psychological approaches to aggressive people: for these you'll need to get expert advice from a specialist in the care team. But it does give you guidelines to follow if you're first on the scene of a situation which includes danger or injury.

If someone's missing

Not all emergencies concern people who are there – you may find that one of your clients has disappeared from the care setting. The first thing to do is to make sure that she is not somewhere else known to your colleagues – make sure, for example, that she has not been taken to see another care professional, or to the hairdresser's.

Make enquiries in the local area, keeping your supervisor informed of the progress of the search and being sure to follow any procedures your care agency may have about missing persons. When you find any information – or, better, find the person – make sure that everyone who has been alerted is told.

As soon as possible after the incident, make a report to your supervisor. Sort out what happened, and think of ways to stop it from happening again.

Health emergencies and first aid

If you find someone who needs help because of an accident or health emergency, the first thing to do is remember to keep calm and observe what's going on – acting too quickly may cause more injury or distress.

Once you've assessed the situation, make sure that the person who has been injured is protected from further injury – by moving dangerously-placed furniture, turning off cookers or taking other simple action to make the situation safer. Make sure, too, that no one else nearby is in danger. If you're in doubt as to the safety of an action, though, don't do it – for example, in the case of electric shock where the source of the electric current might still be live.

The first priority is to get trained help, by sending someone or by using an alarm cord or button. Your first instinct may be to make the person comfortable – perhaps by moving him into the recovery position (see page 70), or putting a cushion or blanket under his head. But this can be dangerous: unless you have first-aid training, be very wary about moving someone.

If you are trained to give first aid, do so. This might include clearing blocked airways by removing dentures; applying bandages to staunch bleeding; covering the person with a blanket to keep him warm in case of shock. Do *not* give the client anything to drink, or administer drugs of any kind – leave that to the professionals.

When professional help arrives, explain what happened as quickly and clearly as you can, and help the professional in any way necessary.

ACTIVITY

Talk with your supervisor about your centre's procedures for dealing with apparently missing clients. Make sure you know:

- whom you should tell;
- arrangements for contacting the police or hospitals;
- the extent of the local area to be searched before further action is taken;
- how a report should be made after the incident.

There may be times when you discover someone whom you think is dying, or perhaps already dead. In such cases, make sure that the immediate environment is safe, as you would in the case of injury, and get help straightaway. Do what you can to reassure people who may be present, and wait until help arrives.

Without moving her, try to make the person as comfortable as possible, perhaps with blankets and cushions. Take her hand and talk quietly. It is often very difficult to tell whether someone is dead or deeply unconscious, and often unconscious people can still hear clearly. Do all you can to comfort and reassure. As far as possible, behave in accordance with the beliefs or attitudes of the person to avoid causing distress. As before, help your supervisor or other specialist in whatever way needed when he arrives.

Afterwards, make the necessary report to your supervisor, following the set procedure. If you need to complete documents or reports, do so quickly while the events are still fresh in your mind. Sometimes you may have to give evidence later in a coroner's court, so make sure at the time that you make a simple, accurate and complete record of what happened, limiting yourself to what you saw and heard yourself.

Events of this sort are bound to happen in almost any care setting. How effectively you deal with them will depend on how well you are prepared for them. In practical terms you can do this by attending first-aid classes, practising applying dressings, and generally having the confidence to take control.

You can also prepare for it by developing a relationship of trust with the people you care for. If your clients trust you, they will automatically help in moments of crisis – and this will do much to ease the suffering of people who are injured and distressed.

2.8 Moving somewhere new

Moving from one setting to another can be upsetting for people in care. There are possessions to be collected, transport to be endured, and perhaps new people to be dealt with. Even a move from one part of a care centre to another can be a major disruption to routine. This is where the care worker can help – not just in making the practical arrangements so that the move goes smoothly, but in ensuring that distress is kept to a minimum and the client is kept comfortable throughout the process.

Other sections talk about going with a client for treatment, and helping the client to move during her stay at a care centre: this section is about more permanent moves, such as going to live in a new wing of a care centre or changing from one centre to another.

Beforehand

THINK...

Write a sentence explaining why you think it's important that the client understands the reason for the move.

Make sure you have all you need for the journey

books and magazines

hot drinks

change and Phonecard for emergency calls

rug

food

map

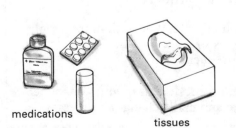

medications

tissues

Unless the client knows what's happening and why, he will be confused and resentful – with good reason, since no one likes being shunted round without explanation. This may lead to longer-term feelings of rejection, as the client may imagine that another resident, or even a member of staff, has complained about him and asked for him to be moved.

Explain to the client what's happening, using suitable language that he will understand. Reassure and encourage as much as you can; if there's a question you can't answer, or if the client is distressed or simply refuses to go, get help from your supervisor.

Some clients may feel able to make journeys unescorted. In such cases, always get help from your supervisor and, if necessary, spend some time explaining to the client why it's better for you to go along too.

Make sure that you have everything you and the client need for the journey. Items might include:

- clothes;
- personal belongings;
- medical records;
- drugs or personal aids needed on the journey;
- something for the journey – a book or toy, for example – to give comfort and reassurance or simply help pass the time.

Make sure that all these items are collected, checked and packed in good time. Aim to get the client to do as much of this as possible, but help as and when needed. This will make sure you leave nothing behind – and also avoid last-minute panics which might be distressing for the client.

Before you leave, help the patient to choose suitable clothing and footwear, and allow plenty of time for him to dress in a suitable but dignified way. If you're going outside, make sure that the client's wearing something warm; if you're travelling by car or ambulance, make sure he has strong shoes. If necessary, help with washing, dressing and using the lavatory – you'll find more help on these in separate sections of this book.

Helping on the journey

If the journey is from one part of a building to another, go with the client at the client's own pace. If necessary, use a wheelchair or other mobility aid. It may help to talk to the client to reassure and encourage – a move is never easy, and human contact and warmth will help a great deal. Be aware, though, that the client may prefer to move in silence, to sort out feelings of unhappiness and loss at the change of setting.

While you're moving, keep a look-out for potential hazards – swing doors, steps, uneven floors, doors opening onto corridors – and do all you can to avoid them. That way you'll arrive safely.

Stay for a little while if you can, to see that the client is safely settled in; and make sure that you complete any procedures to 'hand over' the person to a care worker in the new location. Don't forget to say goodbye before you go – as well as being more courteous, this makes sure that the client won't feel abandoned.

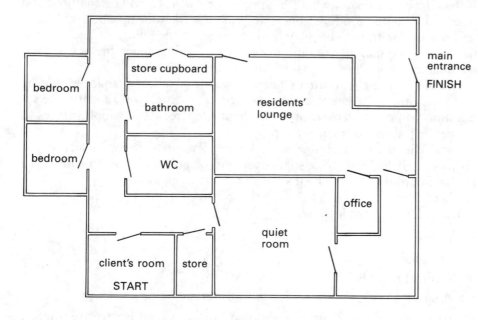

Internal journeys must be planned carefully to avoid obstacles

Sometimes you'll need to move a client by car or ambulance, or perhaps by bus or train. If you do this, make sure before you go that the client is properly dressed – not just to keep warm, but also to keep her as dignified as possible in public.

Practical arrangements need to be made, too. There may be:

- a contact to be made at the destination;
- an ambulance to request;
- a car to arrange;
- train times to check.

Help the client into or out of the vehicle, and make sure she is safe – seat belts or other restraints must be used, and you'll probably need to explain them carefully to the client to get her co-operation in using them.

Try to help the client to enjoy the journey: talk about things you see, other cars or vehicles, cows in the fields, anything you think the client might enjoy or find funny. But it won't always be possible to pass the journey happily. A client may be deeply upset – crying is not pleasant, but it may fulfil a need in releasing emotions of sadness, so be prepared to accept it and be comforting. If it's a long journey, you may need to plan the route to include breaks for food. This will depend on your client's condition – ask your supervisor's advice about this if you're at all unsure.

If you do these things, the move should go smoothly. But it may not: so make sure you know whom to contact in an emergency, and remember practical details like having change or a Phonecard to make calls.

ACTIVITY

Talk with your supervisor about arrangements for moving clients away from the care setting. Make sure you know the procedure for:

- contacting the place where the client is going, to arrange times;
- arranging transport;
- deciding routes and stops;
- maintaining safety;
- making contact in an emergency;
- any special arrangements or procedures your care setting may have.

However and wherever you have to help a client to move, remember always to reassure and encourage. Keep things as smooth and organised as you can: that way the client will arrive safe, without distress and not too exhausted. This will make the move less stressful and more enjoyable for you both.

2.9 Helping people with activities

You may have to look after people who need help in developing and extending their abilities. This might include:

- occupational therapy;
- activities to improve skills for those with learning difficulties;
- physical activities for those recovering from illness or surgery – either with the help of a physiotherapist or less formally.

The nature and frequency of activities will depend on the client and the care setting. They may be an important part of your work, or something that occurs only rarely. Whatever their nature, though, activities can be an essential lifeline for the client – so it's vital that they are organised properly and that everything is done to ensure that they are successful.

Preparations and assessments

Often the proper activity can only be selected after an assessment session in which the client's exact needs can be discovered. This will usually be done by a care specialist such as an occupational therapist, but you may have an important role to play too.

Unless a client understands and is involved with the assessment, the results will not be an accurate picture of his needs, so make sure that he takes an active part in the discussions.

If the client doesn't fully understand what's going on, you might need to get the consent of the client's guardian or legal representative, so you should check with your supervisor who this is and, if there is any difficulty, make sure your supervisor knows about it.

An assessment may involve simple manual tasks, answering a series of questions, or just a discussion of what the client needs and would like to do. Whatever form it takes, encourage the client to be involved by asking questions, making comments and stating preferences.

If you have to help in the assessment, make sure that all the necessary equipment is available, and that it is used in the right way. Generally other members of the care team will advise on this, but you need to know how things should be done so that you can assist in the process. If you have to record any results of the assessment, make sure that they are accurate, and presented in the right way – on a suitable form, for example, or in your institution's preferred format.

ACTIVITY

Talk to your supervisor about therapies and activities. Prepare a sheet giving details of:

- kinds of activity available to your clients;
- care professionals who can provide them;
- assessment techniques involved;
- forms of record-keeping for assessments.

ACTIVITY

1 Make a list of the activity material your care setting has.

2 Then, with the help of the occupational therapist in your care team, your supervisor or other care workers, make a list of the activity and therapy needs of your clients.

3 Now compare the two lists. Do you have equipment to satisfy all these needs? Make some suggestions about what you could add.

Materials and equipment

Any materials and equipment needed should be kept safely and returned to their places of storage promptly after use, with any defects reported to your supervisor.

The equipment should be safe, and suited to the client's needs and abilities, and should also reflect her background and preferences as far as possible. Be aware of special cultural needs, too; swimming in mixed groups will be impossible for clients from some ethnic groups, for example.

During the activity

Before using the equipment with a client, make sure that you understand it yourself. Make sure, too, that the client and the setting are prepared – talk to the client to explain what's going to happen, and rearrange furniture or make other changes as necessary.

Help the client to use the equipment, following the maker's instructions and the advice of the therapist, aiming to help the client do what's required in the care plan. Remember that you're part of a care team here – you're carrying out tasks suggested by a therapist or other professional, but you're just as important in getting things done.

ACTIVITY

Make an appointment to meet occupational therapists or other professionals who are members of the care team involved in activities for your clients. Discuss with them what you should do in activity sessions, including:

- the use of equipment;
- advice to clients while using equipment;
- special areas to watch for during activity;
- kinds of information to be passed on to the therapist.

Do all you can to encourage the client: give constructive advice, and lead by example, using the equipment yourself wherever possible to show your client what's required. Get the person to enjoy what he's doing, and don't push too hard; it's best to get the client to be self-sufficient and dignified in a light task at first.

While the client is using the equipment, look and listen. If anything seems wrong, tell your supervisor as soon as you can. Give the client time to talk about the activity, too: this can be a way of making improvements, and also of increasing the enjoyment gained from it. If you see anything which is limiting the effectiveness of the exercise, tell the therapist or your supervisor so that things can be improved.

ACTIVITY

1 With another care worker or your supervisor, act out a situation in which one of you uses a piece of equipment and the other acts as the care worker.

The user should think carefully about the effects of using the equipment, such as the parts of the body it exercises and any pains it causes. Think, too, about one of your clients and how he or she would react to using the machine.

The care worker should observe very carefully, encouraging and helping the user in as specific and constructive a way as possible.

2 When you've finished, swap roles and repeat the process. Now talk about what you've learned from the exercise, and how it will help you to help clients.

Afterwards

Clear away the equipment and return the room to its usual layout. Make sure that equipment is cleaned, if necessary, and stored safely. Then make sure that any necessary records are completed: the time the client spent on the activity, the level she achieved, and any unusual or worrying circumstances you may have noticed.

Activities and therapy will vary a great deal according to the care setting in which you work, and the nature of the people you care for. It is something which can have a great effect on physical recovery or the maintenance of mobility; it can also be enjoyable and mentally stimulating. Make sure that, as part of an integrated team of care workers, you do all you can to make it as pleasant and valuable as possible.

2.10 Helping people during treatment

Sometimes your work will include being with people while they are having treatment. Such times could be:

- the application of dressings;
- general examinations and check-ups;
- taking specimens of body fluids or tissue.

Where this happens will depend on what the treatment is and the facilities at your care setting. It might range, for example, from being with a client while a doctor takes her pulse in her own home, to helping prepare someone for treatment in a surgery or out-patients' department.

Whatever the treatment is, and wherever it happens, you have two important duties to perform:

- making sure your client is as comfortable and happy as possible;
- helping the professional who is giving the treatment.

Making preparations

First of all, you have to make sure that the person to be treated knows what's going on and consents to it. This will usually mean talking to the doctor, hospital or other professional so that you understand the position yourself.

As far as you can, explain to the client what will happen, using suitable language. Be reassuring, but don't patronise. Do your best to answer the client's questions – if you can't, get help from someone who can.

Then there are practical things. Make sure the client wears suitable clothing – a dress or shirt that can be unbuttoned easily, for example – so that she or he can get treatment easily but still be dignified. You may need to help her or him to use the toilet (see section 3.1). There may also be instructions to follow from the doctor or hospital – the client might have to avoid food or drink before treatment, or take special medication.

During treatment

Your role here is to act as a balance between the care professional and the client, explaining to the client what's going on while helping the professional in any way that's needed.

> **ACTIVITY**
>
> Write a checklist for preparing a client for treatment. Set it out as a series of questions, beginning like this:
>
> (a) Have I explained to the client the nature of the treatment?

Helping the professional can mean:

- passing instruments;
- helping to move or turn the client;
- reporting changes in the client's condition.

Helping the client can mean:

- explaining what's happening;
- reassuring – by what you say and how you say it;
- assisting with movements as required;
- helping with undressing and dressing.

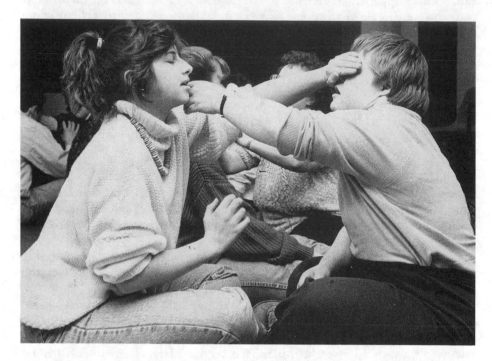

You can see from all of this that helping the professional and helping the client are both essential – often you can't separate the two.

Helping after treatment

Immediately after the treatment there will be practical tasks to perform. Here again, you're there to help both the professional and the client. You'll need, for example, to remove any aids or equipment attached to the client, such as electrodes. Other practical tasks might include:

- labelling specimens and making sure they are given to the right person for analysis;
- taking instruments for sterilisation or storage;
- disposing of body wastes and cleaning spillages (see section 3.1);
- completing any records legibly and accurately.

Sometimes you might need to explain to the client what will happen next. Once again, this involves being a bridge between the professional and the client: as always, be reassuring, explaining the next stage in a clear and suitable way.

You'll also need to help the client physically – perhaps to wash and dry treated areas, and almost certainly to dress. If any equipment has to remain, explain this and reassure the client about it. Remember to be soothing while you do this – not only in what you say but in what you do. If treatment has been long and tiring, a time of rest would help; a cup of tea might be very welcome, too. Make arrangements for transporting the client, and help her to the vehicle (see section 2.8).

While you're doing all this, keep a look-out for danger signs – bruising, dizziness, breathlessness – and get help at once if necessary.

ACTIVITY

1 Talk to a client who has regular treatment in a clinic or out-patients' department. Find out what things are the most helpful when he or she is recovering from the treatment – a brisk, business-like attitude, for example; quiet and reassuring words; a cup of tea.

2 Use this as the basis for your help when you have to accompany this client for treatment, and also when dealing with others – remembering, of course, that they will have different preferences.

In the days following treatment, you might need to help the client carry out further treatment – applying creams or sprays, say, or dressing cuts or bruises. Whatever it is, make sure that you:

- get advice from the professional on how to do it;
- encourage the client to be self-sufficient, but provide sympathetic help and reassurance;
- record what you've done in the way your care setting prefers;
- report any changes in condition to a doctor or your supervisor.

ACTIVITY

1 Talk to your supervisor about the kinds of treatment that are most likely to be given in your care setting. Find out:

- what the treatment is;
- where it takes place;
- what you need to do before, during and after the treatment;
- which clients are involved;

- what procedures there are for keeping records of treatment;
- what arrangements there are for special care after treatment.

2 If possible, go along and observe a client being helped by your supervisor during treatment. Next time, help the client yourself with your supervisor looking on.

Remember that many people you care for will find treatment of even the simplest sort disturbing. Your physical help will keep their discomfort to a minimum: your presence as a voice of reassurance will greatly reduce their anxiety and distress.

2.11 Supporting people's relationships

If someone is being cared for over a long period, it's important that he keeps up the kind of social contacts that we all take for granted. Getting on with other people, looking good, keeping up interests and hobbies, developing relationships of various kinds – all of these are important aspects of life, and you need to do all you can to see that the people you care for can experience them as far as they're able in the care setting.

Looking good

One way of keeping up normal social living is by taking an interest in what you wear. This is just as true of people being cared for as it is for the rest of us. You can help by discussing their appearance with your clients, paying them compliments and showing that you notice how they look. This will help them feel valued as individuals.

Encourage a client to choose her clothes carefully to match the weather and the occasion – if something special is happening, suggest a different dress or shirt. If you can, take time and trouble in discussing these matters. In the case of problems or worries, try to sort them out sympathetically yourself but, if you can't, get help from someone else in the care team – a chiropodist about shoe styles, say, or a dermatologist about make-up. If someone is visually handicapped and can't see clothes, describe to her what they look like.

Sometimes you might need to talk to a client about a prosthesis – an artificial limb. Do so in a clear, factual way, using language the client will understand, or going through an interpreter if necessary. Listen sympathetically to his worries, and be reassuring and encouraging.

ACTIVITY

1 Spend some time talking to one of your clients about what she likes to wear. Get an idea of the kind of approach she has, and then make some suggestions about how she might vary her appearance. Do the same about hairstyles.

2 If you work with children or young adults, talk to them about changing styles of clothes and what they like. This won't always be easy, but if you can get their trust in this, it will help a great deal in building a better relationship with them.

Living with others

Anyone who is in a care setting will want to keep up social contacts and interests. You can help in this by trying to bring together people who have interests in common – be careful, though, not to intrude on their privacy.

Try to develop and extend relationships in a way that isn't intrusive. Helping people to communicate with each other can help in this; arranging outings or providing facilities for activities are other ways (see section 2.9).

As time goes on, people in care will need to develop the kind of give-and-take that's necessary for all of us as we spend more time with other people. Encourage clients to express their own views, but help them tolerate those of others, too. Conversations about news events can help here. Keep a look-out for subjects that are particularly sensitive, though, and try to steer clear of them before arguments get too intense – although disagreements are an inevitable part of life, and there's no reason why people being cared for shouldn't have them too. If disputes do arise, try to sort them out to everyone's satisfaction, thereby keeping disruptiveness to a minimum (see section 2.6).

All of this will help the individual to become aware of his own nature as well as those of others. This is especially important when dealing with young adults, who need to test and experiment with their ideas and attitudes. There may be occasions when you'll need to seek help from your supervisor, but often comments from other people being cared for can be valuable in developing ideas and attitudes, especially for younger people.

ACTIVITY

1 Choose a client you care for who seems to be rather withdrawn. Talk to him about his interests. Try to get him to talk about his feelings for other people in the care setting.

2 Gradually try to involve him in a larger circle of contact – by bringing him into conversations, or inviting him to share hobbies or activities. Be prepared to work hard at this, but be unobtrusive: respect the client's privacy.

3 Afterwards, talk to your supervisor about what's happening, and keep watch on your client's progress.

Sexuality and relationships

People do not stop having sexual feelings just because they're being cared for. You may well be caring for young people whose sexual lives are just unfolding, or helping to nurture those with mental handicaps but strong emotions.

Sexual feelings aren't just a matter of glands; there are emotions to be considered too. In this the role of the care worker is important, but far from easy. How do you decide what is a valid expression of sexual and emotional needs in the people you care for?

There are some clear practical things you can do. First, do all you can to ensure that your own behaviour towards clients can't be misinterpreted; establish a relationship of concern, but at a distance; and respect your clients' privacy except when it's essential to be with them – when they need help in dressing, for example.

Secondly, try not to impose your own views on your clients. For example, people in care may be heterosexual or homosexual, but whatever your own personal attitude to others' sexual orientation, you need to respect this aspect of each client's individuality. The degree to which clients *show* their feelings for each other in front of other clients is a separate matter: but the validity of their feelings shouldn't be in doubt, and these feelings shouldn't be the subject of gossip or amusement.

An important part of your job might be to give guidance on specific areas: the changes the body goes through in puberty; menstruation and any attendant problems; relationships (sexual and otherwise) – these are some of the topics you may need to discuss. If you're uneasy about this, get advice from your supervisor or another care worker: you won't help anyone by giving confused or inaccurate advice.

This applies particularly to topics such as contraception and safe sex. How *do* you discuss AIDS with a mentally-handicapped adolescent who has natural physical needs? There's no easy answer (though there are several specialist publications available).

It is probably easier to decide on the kind of behaviour that's acceptable in public and in private. Your care setting may have guidelines on this: if not, you need to get advice from your supervisor if the situation arises.

ACTIVITY

1 You may find that talking about matters of sexuality with your clients is far from easy. You or your supervisor may feel that it isn't appropriate to raise the subject at all. But in some circumstances it will be essential to raise the topic.

2 Once you've talked this over with your supervisor, talk to some of your clients about the kinds of behaviour they find acceptable in public and in private.

3 Now discuss the same topic with your supervisor. Find out whether there are any set procedures or approaches to follow. All of this will help you to deal with problems as they arise.

4 Repeat the exercise talking about sexual harassment. Ask the clients what they'd do if they thought it was happening, and then – without breaking confidentiality – discuss what they've said with your supervisor.

If things go wrong

Anyone who is being cared for is potentially vulnerable. Sexual abuse of young people in care is a risk of which people are now much aware. It isn't an easy topic, but it isn't one you can fudge.

If you think anything improper is going on, you need to do something about it. Wherever possible, talk to your supervisor or get advice – for several good reasons, it's not something you should tackle alone. This could lead to arguments about facts or evidence; accusations of personal jealousy; and the continuation of the abuse through a lack of authority to put things right.

This goes for unsuitable behaviour in a client, too. You need to explain that certain actions – things said, gestures made, touching, and all kinds of sexual harassment – aren't acceptable. Do so in terms that the person involved will understand, in a manner that suggests you're giving advice, not preaching a sermon. If you've developed a relationship of trust with your clients, this will help: the task will still be difficult, and the client probably won't be too happy, but at least there's a chance that he or she will respect your honesty.

You're not alone in all of this. Remember that you have other members of the care team to call on, and also relatives and friends of the people involved.

Tell the people who need to know what's going on – just as you'd tell them about other changes in health or behaviour in the client. Make sure you know which member of the care team you should approach if you think abuse or harassment is going on, whether by clients or by care workers. Of course you hope you won't need to use them – but it's best to know where to go if you do.

Remember that it's not all gloom, though. Sex should be part of a much wider relationship based on tenderness, sharing and nurture. Intimacy is precious, and can be expressed by a glance or a touch on the arm as much as by a full-blown Hollywood seduction scene – although that's important, too.

People being cared for, whatever their age, their mental or bodily condition, have a right to relationships of the same range and richness as everyone else.

ACTIVITY

Go to your local library and see what material you can find which discusses relationships and sexual problems for the people in your care. Look in magazines on health care for suitable articles. Collect leaflets published by bodies like the British Medical Association and the Department of Health. Keep your collection up to date, and use it as the basis for talks with clients about sex and relationships.

3 Looking after people

This chapter deals with the aspects of caring which are the most direct and the most personal. It covers matters such as:

- moving and lifting;
- helping people to use the toilet;
- personal grooming;
- helping people to eat;
- dressing and washing.

All of these are vital tasks. To do them properly, you need to know certain techniques and approaches. But you also need to remember some key points which are basic to all personal care.

Communication

Whatever you are doing to look after someone, it's essential that you communicate with him while you're doing it. Explain what you're doing, and why, trying always to reassure and encourage in terms the client will understand.

Observing and recording

When you're helping someone with intimate things like dressing or washing, be aware of her all the time. Look for changes in the person's condition – a rash or bruise that wasn't there before, for example. Look for positive things, too – improvements in the person's ability to dress or move an arm, or swellings that have gone down.

Make sure that you record such changes as soon as you can. Do this either in writing, in the way your care agency sets down; or verbally, by telling your supervisor. In this way you'll make sure that all members of the care team know what's going on.

Privacy and dignity

These are precious things to us all – perhaps they're even more precious to someone who depends on others for intimate things. So make sure that whatever you do, you take into account the dignity and privacy of a client.

That means practical things like shutting the door or drawing a screen when you help someone to dress; knocking on a door and waiting for an answer before you go in. It also means talking in a way that's polite and tolerant – encourage firmly, but never bully someone into doing what you want.

Respect the individual

People are not all the same – and we don't suddenly lose individuality when we need to be cared for. Respect the needs of people from different ethnic or religious groups. Get to know the preferences and beliefs of your clients. This will mean that you won't cause them offence or suffering, and it'll help you too. People are far more co-operative with you if you respect their own identities and outlooks.

Hygiene

Intimate personal care involves washing people and disposing of body wastes. Hygiene is of immense importance. Make sure you know the procedures of your agency in this, and that you follow them scrupulously.

Your care agency

Wherever you care for people, you're part of a team. That team can only work if everyone knows what's going on, and if everyone follows the set procedures. So make sure that you know what these are. Talk with your supervisor and ask about where items are stored; what procedures you should follow in certain cases; what other help is available. The sections that follow give specific activities to help you do this – but make a point of finding out for yourself in areas which they don't cover in detail.

Your care agency will have clear procedures about specific aspects of care: how to lift a client, how to wash someone, and how to move someone who is unconscious in bed are all examples of this. If you use the wrong method you might risk injuring the client or yourself – so talk with your supervisor and get them right.

The care plan

Most care agencies work out a care plan for each of their clients. This is discussed in detail in section 1.8.

In general

You may be involved in all of the care activities in this section, or you may not. Discuss the section with your supervisor before you begin, in the way suggested in Chapter 1, to make sure that you approach the sections in the best way and get the most from them.

Some of the activities described here can become matters of routine. Don't let this happen. Remember that you're dealing with individual people who need care and respect just as much as you do. Every so often, try putting yourself in their position; you never know when you might need someone to help you to wash and dress or to use the toilet. Remember that, and you won't lose the sensitivity and concern that lies at the heart of personal care.

3.1 Helping people to use the toilet

This activity has no direct link with your position as a care worker, except in one very important way: it should have made you realise just what an immense difference not having control over when you go to the toilet has on your life and your relationships.

People who need care – whatever their age or nature – are frequently totally dependent on you to help them use toilet facilities. It's a very intimate area of care, and one which can easily be dismissed as trivial: but for the people being looked after, it's something which affects every aspect of their lives.

Getting there

Although people may need help to get to the bathroom, it's important that they stay as independent as possible. There are two main reasons for this. It maintains the client's dignity, and also keeps him or her active, walking and moving unaided instead of depending on care workers. Clearly, independence won't always be possible and some people will need help. So the first thing is to make sure they can get help as and when they need it.

It's important not to intrude on people by asking them if they 'want to go' when they can do things for themselves. But it's also important to give help whenever it's needed. The best way to get this balance right is by knowing the individual needs of the people you care for. The list developed in the activity below will help avoid mistakes.

Remember that people's attitudes to their bodies vary. Many older people find it embarrassing and difficult to talk about their needs: it can often be hard to discover exactly what they want. People might ask for help in many different ways – by asking, by waving, or by using an emergency cord. Make it clear that whatever way they want to use is fine – as long as you can understand what they need. In some clients unhappiness or changes in behaviour may sometimes suggest a need to use the lavatory.

Once the need is made clear, you have to decide what facilities to use. Can the client walk to a bathroom with help? Should he or she use a commode? Or should a urinal or bedpan be used? These are questions you can answer with the help of your supervisor.

If you need to help a client to the toilet, do so following the practice set out in section 3.5. Take care when helping a client to get up, and in guiding him or her. Make sure that you're not going too fast, and talk all the time to encourage him or her and show that you're there if the client is confused.

Using the toilet

First, make sure that the client has privacy – the door of the toilet or other room should be closed so that no one will come in. Some clients may feel shut in if the door is shut, but if you are with them you should be able to allay their fears.

Then make sure that the client is positioned correctly and can reach the toilet simply by sitting. This is important: someone partly undressed, in a confined space with lots of obstacles, can be badly injured when falling.

As far as possible, encourage the client to manage alone. You may, for example, need only to guide him or her to the bathroom. In other cases, you may need to help with unfastening or loosening clothes, and with sitting the client.

Whatever you do, be efficient and respect the client's dignity: try putting yourself in his or her place and thinking how *you* would feel if treated unsympathetically.

When the client is seated, you will probably be able to leave for a few moments – this respects the client's dignity and encourages independence. But if you *do* leave, make sure that the client can call easily for help – perhaps by putting the bell cord on his or her lap.

When you return, ask the client if he or she has finished and, if necessary, help with body cleaning. Take extreme care when helping people to stand; if they need help with using toilet paper, make sure that they are standing securely. But, wherever possible, encourage your clients to do the most intimate tasks themselves. Remember that some faiths have special requirements – washing as well as using lavatory paper is essential for example for Sikhs and Muslims.

While you're helping the client, keep an eye open for bruises, rashes or any other changes and tell your supervisor about them as soon as you can. It's an unobtrusive but important way of checking on people's condition.

Finally, flush the lavatory and help the client to wash. Don't forget your own hygiene needs – wash your hands thoroughly as soon as you can. Then guide the client back to the living area or private room.

Disposing of waste

If a client can't use a flush toilet, you'll need to take special precautions. If there are spills, make sure that:

- you get help;
- the spill is recorded;
- the area is cleaned and disinfected at once.

ACTIVITY

Your own care institution will have procedures for disposal of body waste. Talk with your supervisor and find out:

- where protective clothing is kept;
- where waste should be taken;
- how it should be disposed of.

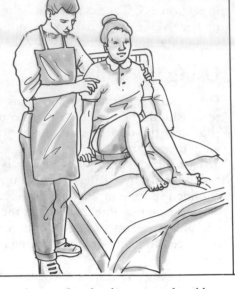

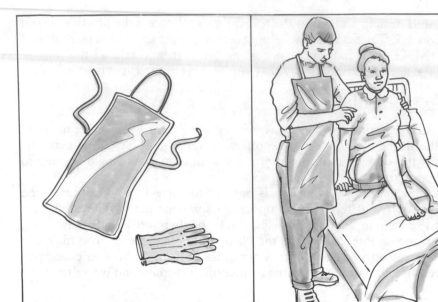

Wear protective clothing (disposable apron and gloves)

Make sure that the client is comfortable and that the immediate surroundings are clean and, if necessary, disinfected

Take waste in a secure container to a toilet or disposal point

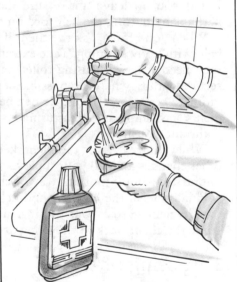

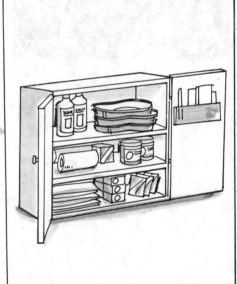

Dispose of waste promptly

Clean and disinfect containers or commode pans

Return the containers or pans to the place where they are stored

Special needs

Generally, helping people to use the toilet can be done quickly and efficiently. But at times you'll need to carry out extra tasks.

Sometimes you'll need to keep a record of the amount of urine passed, or the time of bowel movements. Do this following the procedure your supervisor, or a nurse or doctor, has shown you. Make sure that the record is made promptly – and legibly!

You may also need to report important changes – if a client has difficulty or pain when using the toilet, for example, or if blood is passed with faeces or urine.

All the time, remember – one day someone may have to do this for you.

ACTIVITY

Talk with your supervisor to find out:

- whether you'll need to keep records of this kind for any of your clients;
- how and where you keep them.

3.2 Helping to manage continence

Taking clients to the toilet and helping them to use it is only one of a range of tasks involved in helping people to manage continence – controlling their bodily functions or, when these are beyond control, helping to deal with incontinence in a way that's safe and hygienic and causes the minimum of distress.

Helping with continence

Continence is something which must be seen as a pattern, not a series of unrelated incidents. People's bodies work according to routines – and so, too, do the schedules of most care workers. As a result, it will help to establish a regular pattern of toilet use, both for the client's health and for the smooth running of the care agency.

Most people need to use the toilet at these times:

- first thing in the morning;
- before a meal;
- after a meal;
- last thing at night.

Remember, though, that not everyone has the same needs or habits.

ACTIVITY

With your supervisor, discuss the way that your agency's routine takes into account people's needs in this area. Is there, for example, a policy of helping people to the toilet before or after the midday meal? Find out, too, which people need help and which are self-sufficient.

You can encourage clients to use toilet facilities regularly by talking to them as part of a care team. Make sure you encourage in a suitable way, though – many people are sensitive about such things: think about their outlook and the kind of language they use, and match your approach to theirs.

Make sure, too, that toilets and bathrooms are kept clean and in working order. Report any problems promptly to your supervisor, and put OUT OF ORDER notices on the door to prevent further use.

ACTIVITY

1 Talk with your supervisor about approaches to encouraging regular use of toilet facilities. If there are any clients who have difficulties here, discuss ways in which they could be encouraged to develop a pattern of use.

2 After a week, discuss the subject again with your supervisor to see whether there has been any improvement.

Dealing with incontinence

Incontinence is something that you are bound to come across in your work as a care worker. The reasons for it may be physical or psychological, and will be discussed by doctors, continence advisors or other care professionals: but you will have the responsibility of dealing with it at the most practical level.

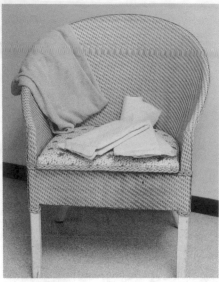

Incontinence aids such as these should be kept ready for use

THINK...

Write down what you think are the *two* most important factors to remember when dealing with incontinence.

Some answers:

1   making sure that it's dealt with safely and hygienically;
2   keeping the client's distress to the minimum.

Fitting aids

If incontinence can be anticipated – if you know it's going to happen – it can be prepared for by using appropriate aids. Plastic mattress covers, incontinence pads and pants and other items will be available from your supervisor. If any of your clients need to use catheters or colostomy bags, make absolutely sure that you know how they should be used before attempting to fit them: always get specialist advice if you are unsure.

ACTIVITY

Discuss with your supervisor what sanitary aids are available. There may be a continence advisor as part of the care team. If there is, discuss things with her, too. Make sure that you know:

(a) what aids there are;
(b) where they are kept;
(c) how they should be used.

With supervision, practise fitting the aids you'll have to use.

When you fit sanitary pads, diapers and similar aids, follow these rules:

- do it in private so as not to embarrass the client;
- always wear protective clothing (e.g. disposable gloves);
- make sure the aid is unwrapped and ready, to save time;
- talk to the client in suitable language, explaining what you're going to do;
- make sure that any lifting or moving is done in the approved way to avoid injury, either to the client or to yourself.

Disposing of aids

As well as fitting aids, you will need to dispose of them when they are soiled. Your care agency will have a procedure for this, so make sure that you follow it at all times. Be sure, too, to wear protective clothing. Have ready a container into which the soiled pads or diapers can be placed.

Remove the aid carefully so as to avoid spillage, making sure that you respect the client's dignity and privacy, and talking to the client to reassure him or her while you do so. Wipe or wash the client – but again explain what you're doing to avoid distress. Watch for any sores or abnormalities while you're doing this.

Put the soiled item in the container and dispose of it – and disposable protective clothing – straightaway. If there are any spills, make sure that they are cleaned and the area disinfected at once. Spills may need to be recorded – check with your supervisor about this. After cleaning up spills, wash your hands thoroughly before going on to other tasks.

When you have disposed of the waste material, make sure that any sores or abnormalities that you noticed are fully recorded in the appropriate place so that action can be taken if necessary.

ACTIVITY

1 Arrange with a supervisor or more experienced care worker to watch him apply an aid of this type. Explain to the client why you're there, and ask whether she would mind. Watch the process carefully.

2 Next time, apply the aid yourself, with the supervisor there to help if necessary.

3 Afterwards, discuss your performance with the supervisor and, if necessary, repeat the task under supervision until you're quite confident.

4 Now repeat the process to practise *removing* a sanitary aid.

Incontinence isn't an easy thing to deal with. Do all you can to avoid distressing or embarrassing the client when helping with it. Try, too, to encourage the client to be independent as far as you can – help and support can often be very effective in curing temporary incontinence, and so save everyone time and distress.

3.3 Helping with hygiene and appearance

Being clean and well groomed is important for most people. As well as helping with hygiene, it makes us *feel* better and happier. This section discusses ways in which you can help people to manage their own hygiene and appearance.

Sometimes, you may meet a client who has no interest in keeping clean. Ultimately you have no right to impose your standards on the client, but her health must be considered. What you do in such cases must be the result of careful discussion between the care team and the client.

Helping people to wash

As this is a very intimate, personal task, it needs to be approached with tact and consideration. You need to be sure of the client's personal needs first – if he can wash without help, don't offend by giving it. Then there are questions of cultural practices – the ways in which people from different ethnic groups approach washing and personal hygiene. These are matters that you must be aware of if they are likely to arise in your care setting; make sure that you discuss this fully with your supervisor if you are at all unsure.

Once you've sorted out the needs, the practical matters need to be settled. As far as possible, let the client choose her own toilet requisites: the right kind of soap can make a lot of difference. Make sure that they are available and within easy reach, too.

When the client is washing, it's usually a good idea to make sure that the room is warm and private – open doors cause draughts and also make the client feel exposed. But this isn't always a good idea. Many older clients feel happier with doors left open a little way, so that they do not feel cut off. Some may quickly forget where they are, and feel shut in. Always remember the needs and preferences of each individual, if necessary getting advice from your supervisor.

Check that the water is of the right temperature. If you're running a bath, remember that many people with poor circulation have a low tolerance for hot water.

When you've finished, take any bed linen or clothes which need to be washed to the laundry area, and make sure that the bathroom or washing facilities are left clean for the next user.

ACTIVITY

Find out all you can about the special washing equipment you have in your care setting. Hoists, trapezes, and special baths with doors or chair lifts all need to be operated carefully: in your work file, make notes on how they work.

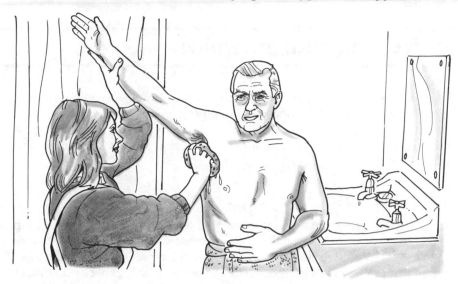

When helping a client to wash, respect his dignity and note any sores or bruises to report later

Helping people to dress

As far as possible, the client himself should choose his clothes. Make sure that they are kept clean and stored within easy reach. Clients should be encouraged to dress themselves, but if they need help, give it tactfully, according to their personal or religious attitudes. Clients may also need help with spectacles or hearing aids – be sure you know how they are fitted, by asking your supervisor.

Clients with prostheses – artificial limbs – need special help. Get to know how these are fastened, and check that they are comfortable and not chafing. The same is true for orthoses – braces, trusses, collars and other support items. Any sores or chafings should be noted and reported to your supervisor. Remember: help the client firmly but with sensitivity, so that her dignity is always preserved.

Helping with oral hygiene

Keep the items for your client's oral hygiene securely, for his or her use only

Encourage independence, but be near; wear protective clothing, and help the client to the bowl or washbasin

Help the client, respecting his or her dignity and noting any pain or sores to report later

Dispose of waste, clean the bowl or basin, and store personal items

3.4 Helping with grooming

Most people feel better when they look better – with clothes in order, neat hair and well-cut nails. This doesn't stop when people need to be cared for: often it becomes even *more* important to their physical and psychological well-being. So helping with grooming and appearance is a positive and worthwhile activity.

Caring for hair

This is something that can give a great deal of pleasure to a client. If you help someone to wash or style her hair, make sure you spend time discussing with her what you're going to do. This will not only help prevent mistakes; it can also add to the enjoyment the person gets from the experience. Make arrangements, where necessary, for a visit to a hairdresser's or for a hairdresser to visit the client.

When you wash and dry someone's hair, or even just comb or brush it, make sure that you do this in the way he prefers. Afro-Caribbean hair requires care and grooming of a particular kind: it is relatively thick, and therefore requires specific shampoos, conditioners and lotions, and styles will need to be thought of carefully, too, to make sure that the client is happy with how it looks. Devout Sikhs believe that the hair must never be cut or shaved, so be sure to talk to the client carefully about hair care and respect his or her wishes. Get special advice about these matters if you are at all unsure.

Talk to the person all the time, and do all you can to avoid discomfort. Keep an eye open for rashes or other abnormalities and report these as soon as you can – either by telling your supervisor or by recording it in writing.

Don't overlook the need to take care of the equipment. Combs and brushes should be kept clean, and reserved for the use of their owner. When you've finished using it, equipment should be cleaned and put away. If you wear protective clothing, it too should be cleaned and stored properly.

ACTIVITY

Prepare a record card with the following information for one of your clients:

HAIR CARE RECORD	Name: *Ms Jones*

Combs/brushes stored: *Bedside cabinet*

Hair washed at *3 day* intervals

Hairdresser's name and address: *Julie Baker*
34 Station Parade

Hairdresser's visit day: *Thursday*

Special shampoos/hair treatments used:
hypo-allergenic shampoo and conditioner

Sometimes you'll need to help clients with removing hair. This could involve helping people to shave, trimming beards, or using hair-removal creams. It's important to do this in the safest possible way – try to use electric shavers, for example, and check that depilatory creams will not have any adverse effects such as rashes or discoloration.

If you have to use a razor, make sure that you use a proper shaving cream in the right quantities to avoid 'razor burn'. Disposable plastic razors are cheap, hygienic and safe. Tilt the client's head back and shave the throat with long smooth strokes towards you, holding the surface of the razor flush with the skin. Then tackle the cheeks, tilting the head away from you and pulling the razor downwards. Finally, shave the chin and upper lip, pulling the razor gently downwards. Afterwards, wash the face and dry with a hot towel; if the client wishes, apply aftershave lotion by placing a little in the palm of each hand and touching them lightly against the cheeks. As before, discuss things fully with the client and make sure you follow his wishes wherever possible. Make sure, too, that equipment is cleaned and stored properly after use.

Caring for nails

This is something which may be excluded from your routine of care. There may be general reasons of policy for this, because of the danger of assault, or specific medical ones, for example if a client has diabetes. As always, check with your supervisor to find out your centre's policy.

If you do have to care for someone's nails, the process may involve cleaning them with brushes, buffers or other equipment, and trimming them with nail scissors or clippers (known as 'nippers'). Discuss things with the client and try to follow her wishes.

Caring for toenails is more complicated, especially for older people. Keep a careful look-out for symptoms of pain or discomfort, and report any changes to your supervisor or to a chiropodist if one visits regularly.

ACTIVITY

Find out from your supervisor what arrangements there are for the foot-care requirements of your clients. In particular, find out:

● the name and address of the chiropodist who is attached to the care team;

● whether the chiropodist visits the clients regularly and, if so, when;

● arrangements for contacting the chiropodist if regular visits aren't made.

Help with clothes

Dressing can be a source of pleasure to people you care for. Encourage them to wear suitable clothes, and take an interest in what they wear. It's easy for people who live alone to wear the same things every day; try to get them to vary their clothes, and to keep up an interest in their appearance. Looking after clothes can also be a source of interest, as well as being an important practical need which you may need to stress to a client.

Clothes should take into account people's needs, but also their likes and dislikes. Wrap-around skirts, elastic waists, open-necked shirts or loose jumpers – all of these will be easier to put on for people who find it hard to move. Bright, fashionable clothes can be very helpful in cheering up younger people.

Take into account special cultural needs, too. Hindu women, for example, may need help in putting on a sari, and may well wear this or shalwar kameez (a tunic and loose trousers) for both day and night. As always, ask your supervisor for help if you are unsure; and remember that for most Asian people clothing has a symbolic as well as a practical function, and that undressing is almost always done in private, so help with dressing may be rejected at first.

Footwear is very important, especially for older people. Talk to your clients about what kinds of shoes they prefer – but get advice from a chiropodist about the kind that they need.

Remember that clothes are very personal things: unless there are very good reasons, keep each person's clothes and footwear for her own use only.

ACTIVITY

Spend some time talking to a client about his or her clothes. Discuss the following:

- what sort of clothes he or she likes to wear;
- what special needs he or she has to consider – difficulty in fastening buttons, for example, or problems in moving arms or legs because of arthritis;

- how clothes are washed and cleaned – for example, who does the washing, or how often items are dry-cleaned;
- whether there are any items the client needs;
- kinds of footwear the client likes, and any special needs in this area.

Just how involved you get with your clients' clothing and grooming will depend on the context in which you see them. If it's a residential setting, then you'll have to help them a lot more than if you visit them in their homes, or see them in a day-care centre. But whatever the setting, make sure that you're aware of two key needs:

- the individual's own needs and preferences in grooming;
- the practical arrangements the care agency has to meet these needs, such as links with chiropodists and hairdressers, and its procedures for laundry and dry-cleaning.

ACTIVITY

1 Prepare a short fact file on the practical arrangements your care agency has to deal with the grooming needs of its clients.

2 When you've finished, think about ways in which it might be improved.

3 Discuss the subject with your supervisor.

3.5 Helping people to be comfortable

A lot of your work will involve lifting and moving people so that they can feel comfortable. If you're dealing with people recovering from surgery, elderly people, or those with physical or emotional disorders, it's especially important that you make them feel as comfortable as possible. Failure to do this can result in physical problems such as bed sores, or emotional and psychological distress.

THINK...

Write down what you think are the two most basic priorities when lifting and moving people.

Some answers:

(a) making sure you don't hurt the client;
(b) making sure you don't hurt yourself.

The first of these is straightforward enough – obviously you don't want to hurt the client. But why is not hurting yourself so important?

Lifting someone or helping them to move is a physically demanding task. It's very easy to hurt yourself by straining your back. It is also vital that you have a proper hold on the client: if you don't, the client could slip or you could both fall – causing further injury to the client and harm to yourself.

Preparing to move

Proper lifting depends on proper preparation.

Before you start, make sure you know how to operate any lifting aids which your agency may have. Hoists, trapezes, stair-lifts, slings, or tail-lifts on ambulances – you must be familiar with them all and be able to use them correctly without endangering your client or yourself.

Check, too, that it is safe for the client to use the aid you have in mind. There may be something in the care plan which prevents it, so make sure before you start. Make sure also that you are aware of the care setting's policy on lifting. Some centres employ a physiotherapist to give specialist training or help: most insist that someone completely immobile should be lifted only by two people. Find out about procedures of this kind as soon as you can.

As well as preparing lifting aids, you also need to prepare yourself. Make sure that you're not wearing clothes which could catch in lifting apparatus or the client's clothing – ties, scarves or other loose garments should be

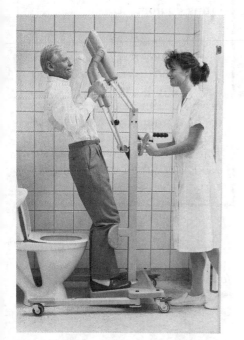

ACTIVITY

1 Discuss lifting aids with your supervisor. Make sure you know what aids your agency has, and where they are kept.

- ask your supervisor to demonstrate them to you;
- make sure you understand the weight limits of each aid;

- use them yourself under supervision;
- practise until you're confident in using them unaided.

2 Then discuss any particular procedures for lifting immobile clients.

avoided. Wear strong, flat shoes, too – you can't balance on stilettos while lifting someone into bed.

Check that you have enough room. Move furniture out of the way. Pull or tie back loose curtains. Make sure that you can *see* where you're going, and that there's nothing you can trip over.

Finally, prepare the client. Explain to him what you're going to do, using language that's suitable but not patronising. Try to get him to help, too – by trying to lean forward, say, or putting the weight on one foot rather than the other.

Lifting and moving

ACTIVITY

1 Ask your supervisor to explain to you the techniques she favours for lifting people. First, observe someone lifting in the approved way; then do it yourself, if necessary with another care worker. Try to get as much practice as you can in this way.

2 Study any posters or health and safety documents you may have which show proper lifting postures and procedures.

As far as possible, lift in the way that the person prefers – but safety must always come first. Try, too, to maintain her dignity: you're not carrying potatoes, remember.

Be sensitive to the way the client responds, too – if she seems in pain, try to stop, or to change your hold. But be careful – don't shift your grip unless you're sure that you won't overbalance and make things worse.

While you're lifting, talk to the client, using suitable language, to help her understand what's happening and not feel confused. Try always to reassure, and to get the client's co-operation.

Afterwards

When you've finished lifting, make sure the client is comfortable. Often non-verbal contact can help: take her hand or squeeze her arm, just to reassure her that everything's all right and you've finished the lifting.

If she showed signs of pain or distress, make sure that this is recorded clearly so that a nurse or doctor can check up later. It might be nothing, but it could be important.

If you've moved furniture, put it back as it was. This isn't only to make things look tidy: it helps people feel secure when physical things are in the usual places.

ACTIVITY

1 Make a list of your agency's lifting equipment.

2 Now make a second list. Write down the name of each client; next to each one list any special equipment which should or should not be used to lift him or her, and any other special notes. Use this as a basis to help you until you get to know the needs of each of the people you care for.

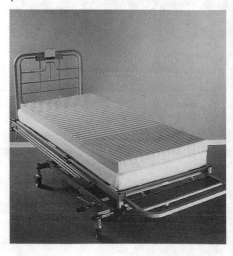

Avoiding pressure sores: a specially-formed mattress can reduce the risk

General comfort

Ask the client frequently whether he is comfortable. There may well be a simple way to improve things – remaking the bed to take out uncomfortable wrinkles, for example, or using a non-allergenic pillow. Many people find nylon sheets uncomfortable, and these can cause skin rashes; others might like a fleecy underblanket to increase warmth and reduce pressure.

When you've discovered any changes which would make the client more comfortable, tell your supervisor and try to make the changes as soon as possible. Pressure sores can start very quickly: it's vital that everyone in the care team is kept informed so that they can all help. And the most important person is the patient: talk encouragingly to get his co-operation with everything that you do.

ACTIVITY

1 Discuss with your supervisor the range of special aids available to prevent pressure sores. They may include ripple mattresses, air beds and similar devices. Find out:

- where they are stored;
- how they are assembled;
- the procedure for using them;

- any special directions for their use;
- how they should be cleaned and stored after use.

2 Observe your supervisor using these aids. The next time they are needed, use them yourself under supervision. Repeat this until you're confident about using them.

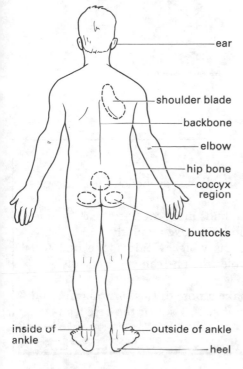

Places where pressure sores are likely

Pressure

Lying in bed without movements, even for an hour or two, can cause pressure sores. These can become serious and very distressing to the sufferer; so it's essential that you do all you can to prevent them from starting.

There are two ways to do this:

- make sure that the patient is moved regularly;
- use any available aids such as special mattresses and pillows.

In situations like this it's important to let the client know what's going on. People confined to bed will quite naturally dislike being moved – so make sure you explain the reason before you make any changes.

Treating sores

As well as checking at regular intervals that the client is comfortable, you may need to apply creams or sprays to prevent sores. Do this by following instructions from your supervisor. Before you start, explain to the patient what you're going to do; while you're doing it, talk soothingly to her.

At the same time, look carefully to observe the client's condition. Look in particular for rashes, bruises or changes in skin colour. Report any changes as soon as you can – in writing, or verbally to your supervisor. It's always important to do this, but with pressure sores it's even more so – they can develop very quickly unless proper action is taken.

ACTIVITY

1 Discuss the treatment of pressure sores with your supervisor. Make sure that you know:

- what kinds of creams or sprays are used;
- what contra-indications (possible side-effects) there may be;
- who can authorise their use;
- how they should be applied.

2 Next time the situation arises, observe your supervisor or another care worker applying these treatments. Then do it yourself under supervision. Make sure all the time that the patient knows what you're doing.

Moving and dressing

Do all you can to encourage patients to alter their position regularly for themselves. If they're fairly active, they won't need much telling – but if they are weak, or even unconscious, then you'll have to help them. The care plan will tell you how often the client should be moved, and give details about sprays or creams.

Always remember to talk to the client about this. Even if he seems deeply unconscious, assume that you can be heard and explain what you're doing.

Moving is often done by pairs of care workers, who turn the body from lying in the recovery position (see the illustration) on one side to lying on the other. Make sure that you get advice on this in each case, though; each person will have different needs, and you should always follow the care plan for the individual. And make sure you lift carefully, in an approved manner; harming yourself will not help anyone.

Make sure that everything is done to keep pressure to a minimum. This may include:

- using special pillows;
- using adjustable headboards;
- fitting frames to keep bedclothes off sensitive areas.

If the client is able to dress, talk to him or her about the kind of clothes which are suitable. An open-necked shirt will be more comfortable than a tie, for example; loose-fitting dresses and skirts which button are easier than garments which have to be put on over the head. Asian clothing is generally looser, but be sensitive towards clients who want to wear items which have symbolic or religious importance. As always, if you have the client's co-operation and involvement this will be much easier.

The recovery position

ACTIVITY

1 Spend some time talking to a client who needs to be moved regularly. This could be:

- someone who's recovering from surgery;
- someone with a disability which makes him unable to move;
- an elderly person with a minor infection making bed rest essential.

Discuss with him:

- what kind of things make him feel more comfortable – kinds of pillows or bedclothes, for example;
- the positions he finds most comfortable;
- the need to help him move regularly;
- the clothes he has which would make him feel most comfortable when he can get dressed.

2 Afterwards, make a note of this information and talk it over with your supervisor or the care team.

Finally . . .

Before you leave the client, make sure that she is comfortable, and safe – perhaps by checking that cot sides are raised and secured. Make frequent checks, and report any changes as quickly as you can. Remember, too, to keep up human contact; being in bed for a while isn't always pleasant and can be frightening, so do all you can to cheer and encourage each person in your care.

Keep an unobtrusive eye on clients in private rooms, by glancing through the doorway as you pass

3.6 Helping people with mobility

Moving around is important. For older people, it helps to maintain general health – to make sure that the body still works – and to prevent sores and other problems arising from long periods of sitting or lying. For young people it's a way of getting rid of energy which might otherwise be used disruptively – playing football is less destructive than smashing windows. And for those who have had surgery, it's a way of ensuring that the body returns to its normal state.

A lot of your time will probably be spent helping people to move: so how do you go about it?

Using mobility aids

Many of your clients, especially elderly ones, will need to use mobility aids of some sort. Sticks, walking frames and wheelchairs will probably be the most frequent, but there are other kinds, like special shoes or even artificial limbs. Helping people to move with these aids is a key function for the care worker but one that has to be done tactfully and correctly, encouraging the client to be as independent as possible.

Before you start

Make sure the aid is clean and properly adjusted for height – a specialist should have done this already, but it's as well to check.

Now talk to the client about the aid. You probably won't have to explain what it does, or how it should be used – a specialist will already have done this. You need to know how it should be used, so that you can make sure the client uses it properly in practice. If necessary, demonstrate – it may look silly, but that can be a good thing, helping the client laugh about it and so build trust.

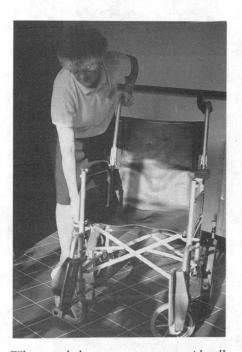
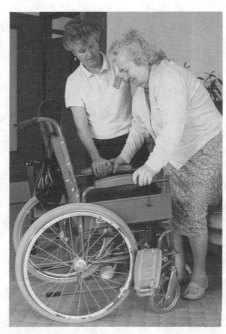
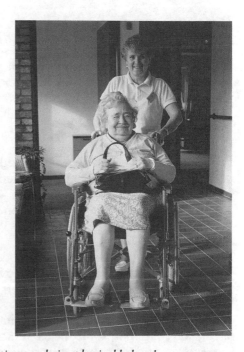

When you help someone to use an aid, talk encouragingly but keep an eye open for obstructions and give physical help when necessary. If the client is using the aid wrongly, tell him or her gently but firmly: incorrect use could be dangerous

---

ACTIVITY

1 At a suitable time, borrow a walking frame from one of your clients. Try using it, under the guidance of your supervisor.

2 Think about how it changes the way you move – the speed you walk at, how you turn round, how you sit down. Think about danger points, too – knocking into things, or keeping your balance when getting up or standing with the frame.

This will help you to demonstrate the frame to clients but it will also do something more important: show you just how it feels to walk with an aid, so that you can understand the problems and danger points from personal experience.

Afterwards

Make sure that the client is comfortably settled – remember, care of the client is more important than care of the aid. Only then, put the aid in its usual storing or resting place. If it needs to be cleaned, do this or arrange for it to be done at a convenient time.

Remember to keep records if necessary. Record improvements in mobility, or times when the client finds moving difficult. This is especially important when mobility is part of a care plan or recovery programme after surgery.

Taking exercise

Exercise can be taken in several forms. It could be:

- a short walk;
- using exercise machines;
- doing prescribed movements to help recovery of movement;
- moving arms in time with music (for those unable to walk).

Whatever it is, the client needs help and encouragement.

Before you start

Talk to the client sympathetically, suggesting different kinds of exercise. Explain why they are necessary, in language that's appropriate but not patronising. At the same time, talk about any equipment that you'd need, or what would be the best kind of clothing to wear.

While exercising

Encourage the client to be as independent as possible, but be there to help if needed. While you're watching a client exercise, talk to him all the time to give encouragement and show how well things are going. If it's a group activity, get everyone involved – 'Come on, Mr Jones, you can do it!'

Afterwards

You may need to keep records of how much exercise a client has done, to show to a physiotherapist or doctor. If so, make sure you do this quickly and legibly in the appropriate place.

If you notice anything wrong – that a client is more out of breath than usual, say, or that someone is reluctant to take part at all – tell your supervisor. And, of course, if someone makes great advances in movement, make sure this is recorded too.

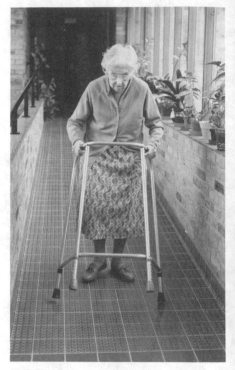

Help clients to exercise safely and appropriately

ACTIVITY

Talk to your supervisor about the facilities available for exercise in your care setting. Make sure you know:

- what activities are available;
- what each client can and cannot do;
- where the various activities take place;
- how furniture or other obstacles can be moved to make the space safe;
- how progress or problems should be recorded.

Moving for a purpose

Some movements have to be made for a purpose other than just getting exercise. People in your care may need to walk to a bathroom, for example; to dress and undress; and to make co-ordinated movements when eating.

Making a start

Before you can do this, you need to know just what the client can and cannot do.

ACTIVITY

Talk with your supervisor about your clients. Make a list showing their ability to move, with comments such as this:

Client	Movement
Mrs Mukerjee	Difficulty in moving upper arms through rheumatoid arthritis; stiffness in fingers makes holding cutlery difficult at times

---

When movement of this sort is first needed, begin by talking to the client. Explain what movements are required, and why: giving reasons will often help. Do this in a way the client will understand, but don't patronise. If you can, demonstrate: get the client to follow your lead, and be encouraging.

Making the movements

Encourage the client to make the movements without help – remember that independence is always a key aim. Be sure to check, though, that the movements are carried out properly, in the right order and – if relevant – according to the care plan or advice of a physiotherapist.

Be prepared to help, and encourage all the time – by saying how the client is managing, by offering advice and by giving praise. Be careful, though, not to talk down – treating someone like a child isn't the best way to get them to use tired or scarred limbs more effectively!

ACTIVITY

In small groups, discuss what else you should do while the client is making the movements.

Afterwards

Using new mobility skills isn't something that should happen only at special times. Make sure that the client gets a chance to use these mobility skills frequently, or to develop them further – by appropriate exercise such as swimming, walking or even playing cards.

Remember, too, to make a note of any special problems or any rapid improvements. Record these promptly in your institution's records system so that they can be incorporated into the care plan. If necessary, talk to a physiotherapist, occupational therapist or doctor about anything which you think is specially important.

You may need to do this at intervals over a long space of time, so make sure that you look carefully and describe accurately to keep a clear record of progress.

ACTIVITY

1 Choose one client who is having problems with mobility and keep a diary of his or her progress over a week.

- Begin by stating:
  (a) the extent of movement now;
  (b) the task aimed for.
- Then write a sentence to describe your first talk with him or her, saying how you tried to help with mobility.
- On each later occasion, write a sentence saying what you did and how the client managed.
- On the last occasion, write a couple of sentences saying how the client has improved.

2 When you have done this, talk with your supervisor about what you did. Mention in particular:

- approaches you used to try to help, including both those which succeeded and those which didn't go too well;
- ways you could increase the help you give to the client in the future.

3 Use the experience you gain from this the next time you have to help a client with mobility.

MOBILITY DIARY

Client's name: _____

Extent of movement now: _____

_____

_____ Date:___ / ___ / ___

Movement aimed for: _____

_____

_____ at (date): ___ / ___ / ___

Notes on first talk: _____

_____

_____ at: ___ / ___ / ___

Progress:

1 _____ ___ / ___ / ___
2 _____ ___ / ___ / ___
3 _____ ___ / ___ / ___
4 _____ ___ / ___ / ___
5 _____ ___ / ___ / ___
6 _____ ___ / ___ / ___

Final achievement: _____

_____

_____ Date:___ / ___ / ___

Signature of care worker: _____

3.7 Helping people to eat and drink

Selecting food

Sometimes there won't be a choice of dishes available. But most of the time you'll have to help your clients select food. This could be by talking things over, or ticking items on a menu form. Whatever form it takes, you *must*:

- know each client's special dietary needs;
- know about special eating practices – for example of Asian or Afro-Caribbean clients;
- be sure that the client *knows* her needs;
- be sure that the client knows what's available.

This means talking to the client and making sure that she understands. In particular, you need to be sure that she understands about special dietary needs, and what she should not eat. Remember the advice given in section 2.1 – use language you know the client will understand, and keep your body language suitable too. If necessary kneel or sit close so that she can see you.

Sometimes you might have to persuade a client to eat food that's nutritionally suitable – or even to eat anything at all. How far do you go? Here you need to rely on your knowledge of the client, and whether he'll be persuaded. If you can't get him to eat, you need to get help – so, as always, knowing whom to contact for help and support is crucial.

Making preparations

Before she eats, you'll need to make sure that the client is ready for the meal. It may be necessary or convenient to take the client to the lavatory – section 3.1 discusses this. You may also need to prepare the client in other ways. Make sure that, if she uses dentures, these are comfortably in place. Check that their use is part of the care plan – it may be that they are not to be used for a while, to avoid the danger of choking, say, or to prevent mouth ulcers from forming.

Your client might be eating in a dining room or in her own room, perhaps even in bed. If you need to help the client to a dining room or other eating area, make sure that you do so carefully, using the advice given in section 3.6. Try to arrange the seating so that people can see each other and talk while eating – social contact is important, remember.

Make sure, too, that the client is in a comfortable position for eating – get help with lifting if necessary. Finally, give the client a napkin or, if necessary, some form of bib or protective clothing.

The eating area, whether bedroom or dining room, must be prepared too. It should be clean and pleasant: nobody likes eating in a dirty or cluttered place. Make sure, too, that all crockery and cutlery is clean, and try to handle it as little as possible.

Serving food

Food should not be too hot, to avoid scalding the client's mouth. Whether you're carrying food on a tray or putting it on a table, make sure that the risk of spilling is kept down, by using the right sort of crockery, cutlery and mats. All utensils should be clean; try, too, to arrange things attractively to encourage the client to eat. Condiments and sauces, where used, should be within easy reach, and in containers which make spilling unlikely.

Place the food so that the client can reach it easily – this will reduce the
risk of spilling as well as making life easier for him. But if the client is
visually impaired, be sure that he cannot scald himself by knocking over hot
drinks or food.

Helping the client to eat

If you have to feed a client, first of all make sure that you have food that's
appropriate to the client's dietary and cultural needs. Make sure that it isn't
too hot, and tell the client what the food is.

Eating and drinking is a very personal thing, so you should do all you can
to encourage clients to do it for themselves. Automatically assuming that old
or infirm people must be fed like children can cause a lot of distress; so don't
assume that they need to be fed unless you're sure that it's really necessary.

If your employer has a policy for health and safety which relates to
feeding, follow it. Make sure, too, that you won't be interrupted except for
genuine emergencies.

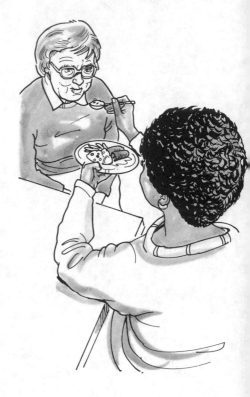

Now make sure you're in the right position. Sit close, so you can reach
both the food and the client without straining or twisting your back: this
avoids spills and also prevents injuries. Protect your client's clothes by using
a napkin or an apron.

It's *easier* to cut the food up first – that is, it's easier for you, but not
necessarily better for the client. Once again, do all you can to encourage
independence: if it means that the meal takes a lot longer to complete, that is
less important than that the client has retained dignity and individuality.

If you do have to feed the client, avoid taking too much at a time: many
people are embarrassed about being fed, and giving them heaped forkfuls of
food will make this worse, and risk the food being spilled or the client
choking. Help the client to wipe her mouth at the end of the meal, or when
necessary.

Always say what you're doing. It keeps up human contact, and makes
things less awkward. You might also need to give the client directions – ask
her to open her mouth, for example, or to raise her head so that you can
wipe her mouth. At the same time, keep an eye open for any signs of
difficulty or reluctance with eating, changes in appetite, or problems in
handling or using cutlery.

ACTIVITY

1 With another care worker – preferably someone
you don't know well – taking the part of a client, go
through the stages of helping the client to eat.

2 When you've finished, reverse roles.

3 Talk about how you both performed; how you
might have improved the task; and what it feels like
to be fed by someone.

If things go wrong

Always make sure you know what to do if the client chokes. If you're in any
doubt at all when this happens, get help – you should have been told who is
a trained first aider in your centre, but if you're unsure, ask.

There might be other problems. The client might not want to eat
something you know he should have to fulfil dietary needs. If you've been
cheerful and helpful in the feeding process, this shouldn't happen too often.
But if it does, persuade, don't force: if this fails, get help.

Afterwards

Collect up the dishes and, if necessary, wipe the table or tray clean. Leave nothing behind which might harm the client. Take the dishes to the kitchen or cooking area. Dispose of waste food properly, following your employer's health and safety code.

If you noticed anything unusual in the client's eating, report it, either by telling your supervisor or by writing it legibly in the appropriate place.

Special needs

Some clients may need to have particular diets, so be certain that you know about these. Any special food needs to be prepared in accordance with the care plan and the religious beliefs of the client: whenever possible, encourage the client to become involved in this to make sure it's done correctly and also to provide an activity of interest. Section 4.5 also discusses special food needs.

Sometimes you'll need to keep accurate records of the amounts of food and drink consumed. Talk to the person you're caring for about this; it will work out much better with his co-operation. Make sure that quantities are accurately measured before you give the client the meal. Afterwards, work out how much was taken – measure drinks in millilitres and food by mouthfuls or grams, or use the system a nurse or doctor has recommended.

Record the amount consumed as soon as possible – you'll probably have been given a chart or table to use for this. Report any adverse reactions, too – it's even more important to keep a check on how the client responds to food and drink when it's being carefully monitored.

ST AGNES Hospital

Hospital no.: *11 111*
Surname: *JONES*
First name(s): *DAPHNE*
D.o.b.: *10.2.20*

DAILY FLUID CHART

Date		Intake (ml)				Output (ml)					
Start time 00.01	Nature of fluid	Oral	IV	Other routes	Bowels	Urine	Vomit or aspirate	Drainage 1	2		
03.30	Normal Saline		500								
04.00	Water	100				200					
06.00	Water	100									
06.30						120					
07.15	Tea	120				100					
09.00	Dextrose saline		500								
10.00						115					
10.30	Tea	100									
11.00	Water	100									
12.00	Water	70				250					
12.08	Tea	150									
14.15						150					
15.10	Tea	150									
16.00	Water	80				100					
17.00						100					
17.30	Tea	150									
18.15	Water	100									
19.00						120					
20.00	Tea	150									
21.00						270					
		1370	1 000			1525					
					Total intake 2370					Total output 1525	Balance 845

3.8 Helping with recreation

The word 'recreation' was first spelled 're-creation': it refers to the ways we make ourselves feel fresh and new by doing something different – a sport or game, or perhaps a hobby of some kind. It's something that's important in most people's lives, and it should also be important for people who need care.

Recreational activities are good for several reasons:

- they keep people physically active;
- they exercise parts of the body recovering from surgery;
- they provide interest and diversion;
- they maintain social contact;
- they keep up mental alertness;
- and, most important of all, they give pleasure at a time when there isn't a lot of it!

Choosing what to do

The first step is to find an activity that's suitable for each person you care for.

To do this you'll need to talk to the client, using suitable language, to sort out what she would like to do. It's the *client* who should decide, remember, so do all you can to make sure that she is given the power to take the decision. Don't rush it – let the client make up her own mind, over a few days if necessary.

When she has thought of something, you'll probably need to get some advice about it. Is this activity suitable for someone in the client's condition? Would it affect other people in the care setting? These are questions which have to be answered, and it's best to do this by consulting your supervisor.

ACTIVITY

1 Talk to your supervisor about recreational activities. For each client, find out:

- special areas for consideration (e.g. a recent hip operation, or liability to faint);

- kinds of recreational activity that would meet his or her needs.

2 Write this on record cards, or add it to your own file on each client.

What each client can do will also depend on the facilities you have, both in the care setting and, for people who are mobile, in the local area.

Of course, not all clients will be happy or satisfied with what's available. Some will want to do things which are difficult practically; others will want to do things which put themselves or others at risk. When this happens, get advice. Talk to your supervisor about it as soon as possible – saying you're worried at the outset may save a lot of trouble later on.

Doing it

The first thing to make sure of is that all the equipment is available, and if necessary is adapted to the special needs of the client. If the client needs help or advice with the activity, either give it yourself or get help from someone who knows about this activity. This is particularly important for sporting activities – you may need the help of a physiotherapist or other specialist.

If you can, keep an unobtrusive eye on what's going on. This will help to

keep risk to a minimum while ensuring that the client is as independent as possible – always a key objective.

Sometimes you'll need to keep a record of what a client has done – if exercise is needed after an operation, say, or if a board game has led to an argument or some unpleasant behaviour. If so, write the record as accurately as you can in the approved place, a record book or other system your care institution will have.

Talking it over

Often, people get as much pleasure from talking about their activities as they get from actually carrying them out. So make sure that people get a chance to do this. In passing, ask them if they enjoyed their swim, or if they had a good game of bridge. This will help build a feeling of being valued, as well as giving an opportunity to re-live something important – a central part of the process of 're-creation'.

3.9 Helping people to use services and facilities

Mobility Allowance, Child Benefit, Disability Allowance, Attendance Allowance, pensions: these are only a few of the benefits people you care for might receive. Getting out to see people about claiming them can be of immense importance in terms of their sheer financial survival.

Then there are other services and facilities that people need to use: libraries, shops, opticians, social clubs. These are just as important – they provide the human contact and independence which people being cared for can so easily lack.

Whether they are in their own homes or in a care institution, people being cared for need help to use these services and facilities.

Getting information

Before you can use a service, you need to know about it. The ideal solution is for the client to find out herself – do all you can to encourage her to be self-sufficient.

Very often this won't be possible and you'll need to find out for her. But make sure that the client is involved – talk about what kinds of information there are, and sort out which ones she could use. Could she, for instance, pick up a leaflet at the post office when collecting her pension? Or could she call in at the Citizens' Advice Bureau on the way to the day centre?

Sometimes, of course, your client will be unable to understand the information, even if she can find it. If you work with people with learning difficulties, for example, finding information of this sort will not be helpful: a social worker will need to be involved to deal with matters like allowances and benefits.

ACTIVITY

Think about one or two of your clients and their present and likely future needs for services. Now think about where you can get information. Make a list like this:

Client	Need	Place to look
Mr Jonas	Chiropody	Health Centre
Miss ffolkes	Income Support	Post Office
Mr and Mrs Owen	Family Credit	Post Office

Once you have the information, talk it over with the client. Spend time on this. If you can, leave the leaflets or other information for him to read, and arrange a time to discuss things a little later.

While you're discussing things, make sure that you ask the client's opinion and, as far as possible, leave the final choice to him. Who has the right to make decisions in cases of this kind is a difficult problem – there are no clear answers. But you should always make every effort to let the client decide – it's part of the aim of maintaining independence which is so important in every aspect of care.

Making appointments

Once you've sorted out which service your client needs to consult, she will probably have to make an appointment to see the person or office concerned. As usual, encourage her to be as independent as circumstances allow – but make sure that certain procedures are followed. Do this by using the checklist.

Appointment checklist

1   Am I sure that the client understands the reason for the appointment?
2   Have I helped the client make the appointment by explaining things in a suitable way?
3   Have I written down the date, time and place of the appointment where the client can consult it?
4   Have I reminded the client about his or her rights to make or cancel the appointment?
5   Have I made arrangements for transport? (Section 2.8 discusses this.)

If the answer to all these is 'Yes', you've covered things well.

Keeping it up

Using services isn't just a matter of making separate appointments to see specialist agencies – though that's important too. It's a matter of helping the client make the most of what's available and of broadening his social contacts as much as possible.

Here are some of the ways you can encourage people to use local facilities:

- stress the enjoyment they'll get from meeting people;
- stress the benefits of the services – new library books, fresh fruit, putting their minds at rest about health problems;
- show clients that they can still help others – by going to a day centre and talking to lonely people, for example;
- show the health benefits from exercise;
- stress the benefits of having a change from routine and getting out of the home.

Encouraging independence is always important. You might do it by, say, making travel arrangements for the first visit, and then leaving the client to make these for later visits – by making a phone call to a car service, if not by walking to the centre without an escort. Your presence at first will give confidence: help the client to build on that by being self-sufficient wherever possible.

But there will be times when this won't be possible. When problems of access or mobility arise, talk them over with the client. If you can't resolve them, get help – ask your supervisor, or a specialist care agency or other member of the care team.

Contact with services is a vital link with the outside world, so don't let your clients break it without a struggle!

ACTIVITY

In your work file, list four ways to encourage people to use local facilities.

4 Organising care

This chapter covers the practical elements of caring for people, either in their own homes or in residential or day-care centres. It covers topics such as:

- confidentiality and security;
- health and safety;
- buying, keeping and preparing food;
- managing life at home.

Each section deals with one particular area of this aspect of caring, and some of these will have more relevance than others to the particular care setting in which you work. Whatever the context in which you work, however, there are key issues and priorities which recur in this part of the book.

Encouraging independence

If you are working with people in their own homes, much of your time will be taken up in encouraging them to do things for themselves. Cooking, cleaning, paying bills – all the routine things of everyday life – may well be difficult for your clients to understand or physically to accomplish.

If the people you're caring for are to cope on their own, they'll need a lot of encouragement. You'll need all the skills of communication and support discussed in Chapter 2, and a lot of patience, too. Often it will seem easier to do the task yourself than to help a client do it. But this won't help in the long run – you won't always have the time to do it, and there are important reasons why people should manage for themselves wherever possible.

Enjoyment and worth

Independence is precious to many people. If we can deal with routine matters of living, it gives us a sense of being in control of our lives. In turn, that gives us a sense of personal worth. For clients who are living on their own and without many sources of success or achievement, simple tasks like doing the shopping or the washing-up can contribute a great deal to a feeling of having done something. Because the feeling of independence is so highly valued, you should do all you can to maintain it in your clients.

Don't forget, either, that tasks of this sort can be enjoyable. A shopping trip can be a way of meeting people and seeing what the town looks like; the process of cooking a meal can be enriching and pleasing in its own right, as well as helping with nutrition. Encourage clients to get pleasure from things like this by talking about them – often planning an outing or talking about a meal can give pleasure, too, and all of this will enhance the sense of worth and purpose that the client gets from the activity.

Hygiene

Physical health is as important as your client's state of mind, and important in this is hygiene. Keeping cooking areas clean, cleaning the bathroom, doing the laundry, disposing of waste food – all of these and others are occasions on which hygiene is of central importance.

Sometimes this will mean encouraging clients to keep their own homes clean; sometimes it will mean cleaning their rooms or living areas in a residential or day-care centre. Whatever the context, remember that cleanliness and hygiene are high priorities in caring for people.

Safety

Allied to hygiene is safety. The various Health and Safety at Work Acts cover the conditions in which places of work must be kept, and you need to be aware of the procedures in your setting and follow them scrupulously.

Safety isn't something you can separate from other activities. It means many things:

- lifting someone carefully so as not to harm yourself;
- not leaving furniture near doors where it can cause accidents;
- opening doors carefully if they let onto a corridor;
- checking that electrical wiring is safe;
- clearing up spillages as soon as they occur;
- keeping fire exits free from obstructions.

These are only a few examples of the ways in which the awareness of safety should be present in your mind. If you see something that looks dangerous, don't assume that someone else will report it or make it safe: do this yourself.

Security

You're not likely to work in a setting which has uniformed guards and locked doors – but you do need to be aware of the need to keep the building safe. Keep watch for unauthorised visitors, and make sure you know about alarms, locks or other devices.

People's possessions need to be protected, as well. You need to know any procedures your setting has for looking after valuables, and to follow them rigorously. Take care of cash, too. If you have to handle it for clients, keep it safely, separate from your own money. If you can, keep a record of what the shopping cost, by writing it down or keeping the receipts.

Teamwork

Practical matters involve just as much co-operation with others as do tasks of personal care. You need to work with many other people if you care for clients at home – health visitors, social workers, occupational therapists, doctors, nurses, and perhaps legal or financial specialists whom you can contact through the local Citizens' Advice Bureau.

Knowing the areas of responsibility of the various people involved is the first step. The second is being prepared to work with them – sharing responsibilities in care, so that the client's interests are always looked after.

Finally . . .

The kind of care described in this part is often the hardest to give satisfactorily. There will be problems over time, and problems over money; and it will often be easy for the practical issues to become more important than the people.

Always remember that the purpose of all such tasks, whether washing-up or sorting out a gas bill, is to make life more worthwhile and more dignified for the person you're caring for. Remember, too, that if at all possible the client should make the decisions, and you should do all you can to avoid imposing your own standards. You may feel that her house is dirty and unsafe: but do you really have the right to change it if the client is happy?

4.1 Confidentiality and security

In any care setting it's essential to maintain confidentiality and security. This means a lot more than not giving information about clients to unauthorised people and locking up at night: it includes a range of other things like looking after vauables, following accepted procedures for listing people's belongings, and even matters such as the Data Protection Act. The precise procedures to follow will be made clear by your supervisor; this section gives general advice on making sure that people and their belongings are kept secure.

Confidential information

Your care setting will have a lot of confidential information: clients' medical records and personal histories, employees' pay records, letters of reference – all of these are essential to the smooth running of a care setting, but are also highly confidential. How, then, do you protect them?

Whatever the procedures, it will be clear that confidential information is only given to qualified people: members of the care team, clients, and clients' friends or relatives. If you don't know who someone is, and what right they have to certain details, ask them who they are. If you do this pleasantly, and explain why you're doing it, the person will value your professionalism and will not be annoyed.

It's also clear that confidential matters should not be discussed in public places, or over the telephone – the only exception to this is when a doctor or other care professional calls for information. The client's own room, or a private office, will be far more suitable for routine discussions.

Confidentiality affects the way in which information is stored, too. If

ACTIVITY

Talk with your supervisor about confidentiality. Make sure that you know what approaches are taken and what procedures followed to prevent personal information from falling into the wrong hands.

you've referred to a confidential file, don't leave it lying around – put it back in its proper place as soon as you've read it.

If your care setting keeps information on computer, it will have to register under the Data Protection Act. Your supervisor or employer will be responsible for this, but you need to know about it to make sure that you're following the regulations.

Keeping clients and belongings secure

In a residential setting, making sure that clients' belongings are kept safely begins when they arrive. Many centres have disclaimers to absolve them from legal responsibility for loss or damage; you should find out your own agency's policy from your supervisor before discussing it with your clients. Make sure that you have a proper inventory – a list of things the client has brought with him. You may need, too, to make sure that his clothes are marked with name tags, to avoid confusion and to make laundry easier – a friend or relative may be able to help with this, but if there is no one else you may have to do this yourself.

Another thing to discuss when clients come to you is their own security. You need to explain, in suitable language, any places where they shouldn't go – kitchens and laundry rooms, say, for their own safety rather than for any other reasons. At the same time, explain any procedures they should follow if they leave the care setting – to go for a walk, for instance, or to see relatives. This can usually be done simply and straightforwardly while you're showing a new client round your centre.

However careful you are about clients and their belongings, it may happen that somebody will lose something or, worse, that a client can't be found. If and when this happens, make sure that you report the incident immediately to the right person, and if necessary write a clear report about it while the events are still fresh in your mind. What to do if a client is missing is covered in section 2.7.

Money and valuables

Clients will often have valuable items, and may also need cash for everyday expenses. Although they may want to keep these with them, you should explain that they'll be safer if kept somewhere more secure – though, of course, they'll be available whenever they're needed.

Items of this sort should be stored in a suitable safe or locked container. This should be done as soon as the items arrive, and a receipt given to the owner. When the items are removed from storage, a record should be made to show when it was removed and who removed it, with a similar record being made on its return. In this way there can never be any doubt about where the items are.

If something does go missing, you should tell your supervisor straightaway so that a proper search can be made. If the search reveals that something's wrong with your system, or if you have any ideas about improving it, tell your supervisor.

Keeping your setting secure

It's essential to keep your care setting safe. The main aim is to ensure the security of clients from attack by intruders – the risk is small but seems to be increasing. Property must be protected, too; the risk of burglary is real, especially if you keep drugs on the premises. Some centres have a single person appointed to take care of daily security, but often responsibility is shared on a rota system between care workers. As well as knowing where your own responsibilities lie, you need to know how the security system

---

John Keble House

RESIDENT'S POSSESSIONS

Furniture

Clothing

Personal items

ACTIVITY

1 Make a list of the procedures followed by your care setting for the care of valuable items. Begin by making clear what a 'valuable item' is – a certain sum of cash, for example, or an item of above a particular value, which your setting decides should be kept securely.

2 Then list procedures for recording, storing and releasing such items. Use this list to make sure you follow the right procedures when you need to look after someone's valuables.

operates. Familiarise yourself with:

- locks;
- security alarms;
- automatic lights;
- any similar devices.

You need to be able to operate them and to report faults if necessary.

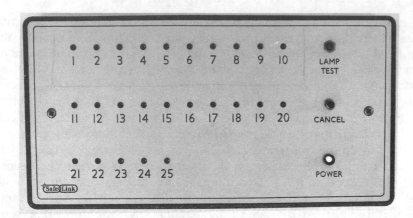

The control panel for an emergency call system

Make sure that you take care over security in other matters, too. Keep keys in their proper location – often a locked key cupboard – when you're not using them. Make sure that stock and equipment is kept safely, and that records of use are up to date and legible, so that there can be no doubt if stock is being used without authority. This is particularly important in the storage of drugs.

Be careful, too, about admitting strangers to the care setting. If you're unsure, ask for identification; if you're still unsure, get advice or say you'll call the organisation the caller says she's from. It may take a little time, but it may save costly and distressing consequences, and no one genuine is going to be upset by good security measures.

ACTIVITY

1 Make sure that you know:
- the order in which security devices should be switched on;
- how and where to turn them on;
- the meanings of warning lights and alarm buzzers;
- how to reset alarms;
- whom to contact if an alarm sounds;
- whom to contact to repair the system;
- where keys are kept and who has access to them.

2 With another care worker, go through the operation of your security systems:
- last thing at night;
- first thing in the morning.

If all this sounds more suitable for a prison than a care setting, don't be too alarmed. Most settings will have a simple and unobtrusive security system – trust is still a sound approach. But it makes sense to be aware of potential dangers, and the best way to do this is by being alert to threats from intruders as well as by having good strong locks. If you know that the security is there, that's one concern off your mind and you can concentrate more fully on the people in your care.

4.2 Health and safety

A care setting is a community: people live close to each other, sharing facilities and concerns. Some will at times be unwell; some may find mobility difficult. In these circumstances, infection can spread quickly; and getting people out in case of fire can be a slow and complex business. All organisations are covered by health and safety laws, too. All these factors make health and safety a key priority for everyone who works in any kind of care setting. Your care agency will have a health and safety policy document: make sure that you get hold of a copy and study it with great care.

Looking after yourself

You can only work properly if you yourself are healthy and protected from hazards. This means taking precautions which you'd probably take anyway, but taking them in a methodical, professional way. It means:

- wearing protective clothing – for example, gloves when washing people with infections, especially if you have cuts or scratches;
- washing hands or other parts of the body that have come into contact with clients who have infections.

ACTIVITY

Give two or three examples of situations where these practices might be needed in your care setting. Set them out like these examples:

Situation	Protective measures
Bathing a client with sores	Wear plastic gloves and apron
Disposing of body wastes from bedpans, etc.	Use appropriate containers; wash hands thoroughly

---

Caring for your own safety means knowing the correct way to go about certain tasks. Lifting clients wrongly can cause serious back injury; so make sure that you know how to do it, and get help if necessary, before you do something that could have long-term consequences.

Using equipment also needs care. Chair lifts, trapezes to ease entry into baths, tail-lifts on buses, and even fairly simple electrical devices such as ripple mattresses all need to be used in accordance with the manufacturers' instructions. Make sure that:

- you know how to use each item properly;
- you get advice if you need it.

In some settings, specialised equipment may pose special dangers. If you need to take patients for X-rays, for example, you must protect yourself from the risk of radiation. In cases like this there will usually be clear guidelines; for your own safety, follow them.

ACTIVITY

With your supervisor or employer, make a list of the equipment in use in your care setting. Next to each item, note down special precautions to take when using it.

Item	Precautions
Chair lift	Avoid lifting clients onto chair alone; this may damage your back through having to turn the client.

If anything does go wrong, or if you think you may have an infectious disease, you must report it. If you go to work with flu, feeling rotten but not wanting to let people down, you'll probably do more harm than good: infection spreads quickly in an enclosed community, and soon many others will be ill.

Not only accidents to others but also accidents to yourself should be reported. Do this accurately, legibly and immediately in the way preferred by your centre. You may need the evidence of this record later on; and your action may stop other people from being put at risk.

Looking after others

As the whole of your job is concerned with caring for people, being aware of their need for safety isn't something you can keep separate from the whole range of other tasks: it's something that needs to be there at the back of your mind all the time.

Some aspects of this are sound common sense. Making sure that furniture isn't awkwardly placed, or that electric cables don't run across corridors, is something that will become a reflex action. So, too, will using equipment safely and in accordance with the instructions.

Keeping a check on the health of the people you care for is something you'll be involved in as part of the care team. This will involve working with other professionals in a range of ways – checking temperatures, monitoring fluid intake, and helping to change dressings may all form part of your work. When carrying out these tasks, make sure that you wear the necessary protective clothing and keep your hands clean. This is not only for your own health, but to avoid cross-infection – passing an illness from one client to another.

Just as you need to report accidents or risks to yourself, you need to report hazards or accidents to others, too. If you think something's unsafe, don't assume that someone else has reported it: be sure, and do it yourself.

ACTIVITY

1 Talk to your supervisor about health and safety in your care setting. Collect as much information about it as you can.

2 When you've thought about health and safety, talk again to your supervisor. Discuss possible improvements or areas of concern. This could form the basis of regular meetings to improve health and safety.

3 Get the clients involved, too: in a residential care setting, this would not only increase safety-awareness, it would also provide a valuable interest for some clients.

Fire precautions

Your care setting will have clear procedures to follow in case of fire. The first thing to do is to make sure you know what *you're* supposed to do.

There are clear practical considerations to follow. Make sure that main routes out of the building are kept clear. Doors shouldn't be obstructed, for example by dustbins outside or parked wheelchairs inside. If you see any faults in an emergency door or an alarm system, report them straightaway.

As soon as the fire alarm sounds, do what you've been instructed to do in the prearranged procedure. Usually it will be to help the clients to a place of safety, quickly and calmly. While you're doing this, reassure the clients to gain their co-operation and make them feel secure.

Once you're safe outside the building, check that everyone is there. Only go back into the building if it's essential for a client's safety; otherwise, follow the instructions of your supervisor or of fire or emergency staff when they arrive.

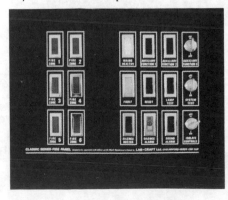

A fire-alarm control panel

ACTIVITY

Discuss with your supervisor the procedure for evacuating the building in case of fire. Make sure you know:

(a) the procedure for giving the alarm;
(b) the signal for a fire or smoke alarm;

(c) who is responsible for contacting the emergency services;
(d) what you are expected to do, and how this fits in with what others are doing;
(e) where you assemble.

Make sure you know how to use the fire extinguishers. Reading the instructions isn't enough: arrange for a practice or, better still, a demonstration by the manufacturers.

Although you need to know how to react in a fire, it's just as important to prevent one from starting. Make sure that smoking – if it's allowed at all – is done only in safe places. If open fires are used, light them safely and keep them guarded and under control. If any materials are inflammable, keep them safely – out of sunlight and at the proper temperature.

If anything seems like a fire risk to you, make sure it's reported. This may not always be easy – it may mean telling residents not to smoke in certain places, and causing anger and resentment. If you do have to do this, make sure that you report your action clearly and legibly in the usual way.

ACTIVITY

1 Find out whether there is a team member with special responsibility for fire precautions and fire drills. If there is, talk to him or her and make sure you understand procedures fully.

2 Once you're confident that you understand what to do in a fire, take part in a fire drill. Make sure that evacuation is carried out fully and quickly.

3 Afterwards, talk with your supervisor, other care workers and if possible your clients about how the drill went. Make a list of things which weren't right, or which could be improved. Put them into practice at the next fire drill.

4.3 Ordering and keeping stock

Making sure that items of stock are kept properly, in good order and in the right places, may not seem something of vital importance in a care setting – but it does have important implications. Running out of surgical dressings could cause a wound to become infected; running out of disposable plastic gloves could cause infection to spread. Even more basic things like soap and toilet paper are essential to maintaining a clean and healthy setting for your clients. For this reason, keeping an eye on stores of materials such as these is an essential part of your work as a care assistant.

Keeping stock

Keeping an eye on stock begins when it arrives. You need carefully to check what's delivered against a delivery note or invoice, to make sure that what you've got is what you asked for. You also need to check that the goods are in proper condition – no split packagings for sterile dressings, no leaking bottles, no faulty goods. Prepared foods must not be kept beyond the 'best before' date printed on the packaging. Check daily for such items: if you find any, put them in a waste bin or, if this is impossible, label them clearly DO NOT USE.

Your care setting will have its own procedures for checking-in goods, and reporting things that aren't as they should be. Make sure that you know them, and can report discrepancies and faults straightaway. This will not only save money – it may also prevent infection.

Once you've checked the stock in, it needs to be stored properly: at the right temperature, and in the right place. You may need to keep stocks at different places, so that the items are ready for use. Make sure, too, that stock is properly rotated – used in the order in which it arrives, so that nothing gets left at the back of the cupboard.

Keep an eye on levels of stock. Most items will be ordered regularly, but if something gets low, talk with the people who use it to make sure that the pattern of ordering is changed. That way, you won't ever run out of supplies.

Finally, if anything goes wrong – if some stock isn't delivered, or some items are faulty – make sure that you report this to your supervisor so that things can be put right.

ACTIVITY

Talk to your supervisor about ordering procedures and stock levels in your care agency. Make sure you know:

(a) who orders stock;
(b) who checks it in;
(c) where things are kept;
(d) how you report problems or faults with stock.

Looking after equipment

As well as stock, you may need to look after various pieces of equipment and make sure that they are kept safe. This might include:

- wheelchairs;
- walking frames and other mobility aids;
- special mattresses;
- collars, braces and other aids;
- instruments to be used by other members of the care team, such as chiropodists and physiotherapists.

Whatever the equipment or instruments are, make sure that they are stored safely when not in use. When they are needed, be sure to use them properly, following the instructions so that they are not damaged and cause no risks for the users.

If any faults occur, these should be promptly and fully reported in writing. The equipment should be clearly labelled DO NOT USE, and placed somewhere where it will not cause an obstruction, and won't be picked up by a client who can't see the label. Regular servicing and maintenance should keep faults to a minimum: make sure that you know whose responsibility it is to arrange for this.

ACTIVITY

Talk with your supervisor about equipment and special instruments. Make sure you know:

(a) what equipment of this sort your care centre uses;
(b) how and where such equipment is stored;
(c) what maintenance it needs, if any;
(d) what to do in case of faults or breakages.

Moving materials

Sometimes you'll need to move stores or equipment from one location to another. Make sure that you do so safely, using the proper containers. Specimens and other medical materials will have to be moved in sterile containers, so make sure you know where these are kept, and be scrupulous about cleanliness. Always label containers fully. This is particularly important if you're moving drugs or medical items.

When you have moved the material, make sure that the person taking charge of it knows it has arrived. You may need to get a signature for the receipt of drugs; be sure that you carry out the necessary paperwork so that an exact record is kept at all times of where the items are. This is not only important for the security of medical items; it also helps to prevent waste and confusion.

ACTIVITY

Get to know, with the help of a supervisor or another colleague, what the arrangements are for the transfer of items in your care setting. Familiarise yourself with forms and procedures so that, if you need to transfer medical products, you can do so quickly and efficiently.

4.4 Domestic duties

If you work in a residential or day-care setting, your job may well include duties such as cleaning, bed-making and washing-up. These tasks are essential to the smooth running of a care setting, and also have much to contribute to the health, safety and general comfort of both clients and care professionals. Even though they may appear dull, routine tasks, they are important, and need to be seen as part of the larger aim of providing a healthy and attractive setting in which people can be cared for.

If you visit clients in their homes, you may also have to carry out duties of this sort, but it's more likely that you'll need to encourage them to carry them out themselves. Advice on this is given in section 4.7.

Cleaning and washing-up

Before you start, make sure that your cleaning methods follow the preferences of the client or care setting, and the appropriate priorities for what is cleaned first or most often. Keep the living areas free from dust and regularly vacuumed; make sure baths, sinks and lavatories are clean and disinfected.

While you're cleaning, try to cause as little disturbance as you can – people in care will often find noise and activity distressing. Take care to avoid damaging furniture and fittings; and when you move items, always return them to positions where they won't cause hazards. Finally, if you find anything that's badly worn or in a dangerous state, make sure that you report it for repair.

Washing-up in a care setting will need greater care than washing-up at home, because of the larger quantities of items that may be involved and because of the need to prevent the spread of infection. You need, too, to be aware of the provisions of current legislation, such as the Food Safety Act 1990 and the Food Hygiene Regulations, and to follow their provisions.

Make sure that dirty items are correctly stacked, and that the instructions for washing-up liquids are followed. Wash the items in a suitable sequence – usually the cleanest and most fragile first, with cooking utensils last. Make sure that items are rinsed to remove washing-up liquid before drying. Keep damage to a minimum by handling items carefully.

Afterwards, store items in the correct places and report any damage that has occurred.

ACTIVITY

1 Spend some time in the kitchen of your care setting. Get to know where cleaning liquids, brushes, dusters and other cleaning items are kept. If necessary, look at any items you're not familiar with to make sure you know how to use them.

2 Ask your supervisor about cleaning procedures. Make sure you are familiar with any special approaches for your care setting. Talk, too, about legal requirements, and make sure that you follow them fully when carrying out domestic duties.

Making beds

Your care setting may have special procedures for stripping and making beds. This may, for example, be done by care workers in pairs; and there may be special trolleys for dirty linen.

Following these procedures, begin by stripping the bed of dirty or soiled linen, if necessary wearing special clothing to protect yourself from body wastes. Take dirty linen to the laundry area as soon as you can, to avoid

ACTIVITY

Talk to your supervisor about procedures for bed-making. Find out:

(a) where soiled linen is put before washing;

(b) where clean linen is kept;

(c) procedures for disposing of soiled linen and for cleaning mattresses;

(d) where mattress protectors are kept;

(e) the method of bed-making that is used;

(f) how often you should turn mattresses.

ACTIVITY

With the help of your supervisor, prepare a single page of notes on the heating arrangements for your care setting. Show:

(a) the kind of heating;

(b) the source of fuel;

(c) maintenance intervals;

(d) the operating instructions;

(e) emergency procedures and contacts.

further soiling. Make sure, too, that a mattress which has been soiled is cleaned, and dried or changed before the bed is remade.

When you make the bed, do so in the way the client prefers, using mattress protectors or other hygiene devices as necessary. Remember to turn the mattress over at regular intervals so that it wears evenly. If there's anything wrong with the mattress, bed or bedclothes, report this so that the damaged item can be mended or replaced.

If a client is still in the bed when you make it, get help to ensure that he is lifted correctly (see section 3.5) and without distress.

Heating arrangements

The exact nature of the duties here will vary with the kind of heating system your care setting has. If you're working in a client's home, things are rather different: section 4.8 discusses this in more detail.

Heating and ventilation in residential homes are covered by various Registration Acts. If you are to be involved with operating heating systems, make sure that you understand the legal requirements which affect your centre.

If you work in a centre with an automatic system, make sure that time switches and temperatures are properly set to provide comfortable temperatures throughout the day. If you use gas or electric heaters, make sure they are properly switched on, properly guarded and switched off when not needed. If an open fire is used, lay and light it so that it burns well but without smoke. Make sure that it's properly guarded and regularly checked and made up with the right fuel when necessary.

You'll also need to be aware of the fuel supply and possible problems. Make sure that proper supplies of fuel are available: this will range from knowing how to use a slot-meter to arranging for a delivery of central-heating oil. Be prepared for supply failures, too – open fires may help if the electricity or gas supply is interrupted. Take special care over using portable oil or liquid-gas heaters, however; if there is any possibility that someone might fall against one, don't use them.

Safety is always a main aim when dealing with heating. Make sure that proper ventilation is provided, and that all gas, electric and other heaters are safe. Have central-heating systems regularly checked and serviced; and be sure to report any faults as soon as they occur, in the manner preferred by your care setting.

Safety

Each of the earlier sections has mentioned the need for safety in the care setting, and it's discussed again in section 4.7. But it can't be stressed too much that safety is something you should always be aware of in your work as a care worker.

When you use electrical equipment of any kind – from a hairdryer to a cooker, from a washing-machine to a vacuum cleaner – make a point of checking that the cord is properly connected to the plug and that there is no fraying. If something doesn't operate at once, don't just fiddle with the wire in the plug; switch off, and get specialist help. Don't attempt to put things right yourself: it's not part of your job, and doing it wrong could cause considerable legal problems if an accident results.

If there's a fault, report it to your supervisor, or record it in a day book or other record. Write a clear label saying DO NOT USE and attach it to the faulty item, to prevent further damage. This will avoid a simple fault turning into a major accident.

4.5   Preparing food

Why food matters

Food is important to most of us. But if we are ill, confused or unhappy, it perhaps becomes even more important – as a way of cheering ourselves up, or even as a social occasion if we can eat with others.

Eating food that we don't like, or food which is against our beliefs or customs, can seem like a further loss of independence – something which older people in care, in particular, will be unhappy about.

On top of that, there are all the dietary reasons – a good, balanced diet is essential for a life as healthy as possible within the client's own circumstances.

What clients need

People who need care may need special diets. So the first thing you must find out is what these diets are, and what things your client should and shouldn't have.

Talk with your clients about what food they like, and what they should or shouldn't eat – no pork for Jews, halal meat only for Muslims, and fish on Fridays for stricter Catholics are three examples. It might help to talk to relatives or other visitors, too.

Don't forget to stress the need for a good, balanced diet, regardless of the client's special needs. Advice on healthy eating can be gained from a number of sources – try to get hold of booklets and leaflets on good eating, and discuss them with your client using appropriate language.

ACTIVITY

With another care worker, talk about why food is important for people in care. Then jot down a short list of points.

ACTIVITY

1 Talk to one of your clients about the sort of food he or she likes or needs. Record his or her answers.

2 Prepare a set of record cards, with one for each person.

Name:	
Food liked:	*Food needs:*
Food disliked:	*Food allergies:*

Preparing food

Your job may or may not include preparing food for clients. If you work in a day centre, for example, you may only need to make hot drinks; if you visit elderly people in their own homes, then you might have to prepare meals.

Always try to encourage people to be self-sufficient: in this case, it not only increases their independence, but can give them enjoyment and a sense of achievement in preparing their own meals. Talk to them about how they can store food hygienically, too, and remind them that things don't keep for ever even in a refrigerator.

If you have to prepare food, make sure you follow proper precautions for hygiene and safety. Wear protective clothing, and make sure that the food preparation area and the utensils are clean. When you've prepared the food, dispose of the waste carefully. Clean utensils and wipe surfaces with detergents, and put the utensils back where they are kept.

ACTIVITY

Talk with your supervisor about the food needs of your clients. Take along the record cards you've prepared, and discuss how you can best meet the needs within the limits of your care setting – cost, time, equipment and other practical considerations.

4.6 Organising care at home

When clients leave your care to return home, they need special help. Facilities for care, care needs, and available services all need to be discussed, not only with the clients but with their families and friends. Knowing how to do this is an important part of your skills as a care worker.

Preparing to move

The decision on when a client is to leave care and return home can be made in different ways. The care team can decide in principle that the time is right; or the client, her relatives, and anyone else involved can get together and talk about things.

Your care setting will have its own procedure here, but whatever it is, one thing is vital: the client, relatives and anyone who may be involved in giving care must be consulted.

You need to discuss the client's needs with the relatives, and the practical implications these will have. In some cases, living accommodation may need to be modified to allow the client to sleep downstairs, say; in others, special techniques will need to be learned by the relatives to help care for the client.

Whatever the details, make sure that the client and relatives understand the client's care plan (see section 1.8). Give them plenty of time to think about things and ask questions. A major part of your role here is to dispel fears and anxieties – so you'll need all the communication skills discussed in Chapter 2.

Practical points need to be covered too. You – or someone from your care setting – will need to make sure that any aids or equipment will be made available to the client, along with information on how to use them. This could range from the loan of a walking frame to the regular delivery of oxygen cylinders, so arrangements must be made thoroughly and in good time.

When you have discussed all of the points, you may feel uncertain or unhappy about the client's abilities to cope at home. Are the facilities adequate? Can the relatives supply the necessary care? If you have any doubts like these, you must discuss them with your supervisor or the relevant member of the care team.

When the client leaves, encourage him and his relatives to keep in touch and to ask for help or guidance if and when they need it. Try to make clear to them that you're still there to help: often just knowing that there's someone to call on can be a great source of comfort in what at first will probably be a difficult situation.

ACTIVITY

With the help of your supervisor, prepare a fact file on clients moving to home care. Include in it details of the following:

(a) the procedure for deciding on discharge of clients;

(b) the names of people to contact for advice on special needs and equipment at home;

(c) the names of care team members in the area of the client's home;

(d) the procedures, if any, for carers to contact your care setting for advice when the client has returned home.

Sorting out the needs

When a client leaves, you need to know exactly what she will need in the new setting.

The most wide-ranging implications will be for the design of the client's home. It may need extensive changes, such as:

- a downstairs bathroom;
- a chair lift;
- wheelchair ramps and widened doorways for access.

If such things are needed, you need to contact the member of your care team who liaises with local authorities to provide grants, and who provides advice on structural alterations needed.

Changes may be more minor, though. A client may need grab-rails near a bath or lavatory, or a device which flashes the lights when the doorbell rings.

Special equipment may also be needed, as mentioned earlier. For this and for any structural changes, you need to make sure that the client and her relatives know what is involved and how the equipment should be used, stored and maintained. If necessary, demonstrate the use and maintenance of the equipment to client and relatives, in a direct, appropriate way.

If anything is wrong – if, for example, a walking frame is the wrong kind, or if a client has difficulty using a new fitting – make sure that you tell your supervisor or the right member of the care team. Remember that even the most perfect equipment is only useful when it meets the needs of the client and she is happy using it.

ACTIVITY

Extend your fact file by compiling details on these matters:

(a) the name of the person to contact about any structural changes needed in clients' homes;

(b) the name of the person to contact about the loan of special equipment;

(c) the department or person to contact about local authority grants;

(d) details of financial matters such as Attendance Allowance payable to carers.

Helping the carer to care

People who find themselves in the position of having to care for a relative may be anxious and confused. They may feel that they are unequal to the task; they may feel guilty that they cannot do more; and they may resent having to sacrifice their independence.

Generally speaking, people in this position will get specialist advice from doctors and nurses, but a lot of the practical help will come from care workers who have come to know the client's needs thoroughly over a long period.

Talk carefully and thoroughly to the carer, explaining the client's needs in language appropriate to the carer. Encourage him to ask questions and voice doubts and fears, so that the subject is covered thoroughly.

Don't rely on just talking, either: *show* the carer what needs to be done, and let him carry out the tasks while you're there, to build confidence. If he has visited the client regularly you'll know him anyway, and this will encourage trust between you. You will probably have tried to involve the carer in looking after the client, so the change won't be abrupt and sudden.

As well as explaining what to do, talk about how the carer can get help – through a health centre, a physiotherapist, a community psychiatric nurse, or some other member of the local care team.

Talk to the carer about the possible need to establish a bond with the client, too. Building a relationship of trust on both sides is important: don't assume that, because carer and client are related, they have an effective, trusting relationship. The sections on communication in Chapter 2 will be useful here.

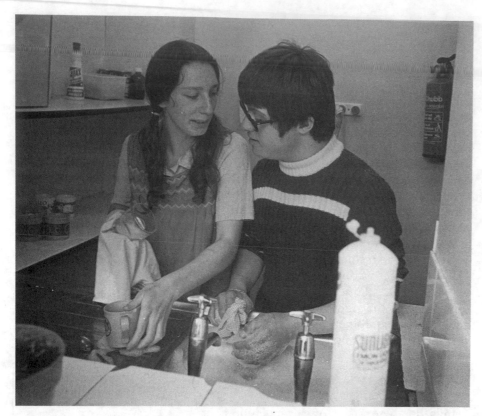

As you talk with the carer, watch for how well he is coping. If you see signs of strain or uncertainty, make sure that you report these, either to your supervisor or to the appropriate member of the care team. Every carer has his limits, and dealing with pressure when it arises is important for the emotional and physical health of everyone involved.

ACTIVITY

1 Work in pairs, with another care worker. First, think of a family member or relative of your own. Consider what would happen if, for some reason, he or she had to be looked after by you at home. Think about the implications for:

(a) your relative – the 'client';
(b) the practical arrangements of your own life;
(c) your family's life;
(d) practical household needs;
(e) the emotional needs of your relative, your family and yourself.

2 With a colleague, talk over what you think would be the most difficult aspects of practical care of this sort. There's no need to invent an actual disability – your skills as a care worker will help you to deal with the practical elements. The purpose here is to explore how you would *feel* in such a setting and how you would cope with the emotional and psychological pressures.

3 When you have discussed things fully, exchange roles with your colleague and discuss the implications for his or her life of a similar event.

4 Use the experience you gain from this when helping clients' relatives to cope with the process of becoming full-time carers.

4.7 Helping people to keep their homes safe and clean

Keeping a home clean isn't only a matter of personal preference. Cleanliness prevents the spread of germs and infections, and also cuts down the risk of accidents. Helping with cleanliness improves the client's living environment and also makes it safer and healthier.

This doesn't mean, though, that you should impose your own standards of cleanliness on a client. If she is happy to live with a certain amount of dirt, that's a personal decision. Knowing when to intervene and try to bring about change is a difficult matter which comes when experience: as always, if you're in doubt about whether the client's right to behave as she wishes or that her safety comes first, talk to your supervisor or get expert advice.

Keeping clean

The exact nature of your job will decide the limits to which you're expected to go in helping a client keep clean and safe at home. Generally, though, the role of the care worker is to advise and encourage, rather than actually to carry out cleaning.

It may be best to begin by encouraging a client to care for his clothes, keeping them in good order and maintaining a tidy appearance. This could then move onto personal possessions. Since these can often be a source of interest and amusement, this is something to be encouraged. Collections of tiny china frogs, postcards, stamps – anything which offers a degree of amusement and stimulus should be encouraged, and keeping them in an orderly way can help with mental orderliness too.

In practical terms the largest need will be keeping the home clean. Encourage the client to buy suitable cleaning materials, and to keep them safely – not where they might be confused with food and drink, or where damp or heat would damage them. Kitchen, bathroom and lavatory are especially important here for health reasons, but living and sleeping areas should be looked after too.

This kitchen contains hazards to safety and to health – but if you correct these problems you remove the client's independence. Discuss with your supervisor what you would like to change, and how you would talk about these changes with your client

Safety is important during cleaning. Make sure the client's cleaning equipment is safe – no fraying wires on vacuum cleaners, for instance – and that cleaning itself is done safely; bowls and buckets must not be left about for people to step in or trip over. Watch for hygiene, too. Make sure that the client has a proper system for disposing of garbage and waste food, and that food preparation areas are kept clean and disinfected.

Encourage the client to report any breakages or difficulties, and to get damage repaired as soon as possible. If problems arise, record them clearly in the manner followed by your care agency – as always the rule here is: if you can't help, ask someone who can.

ACTIVITY

1 Think of a client whom you visit regularly. Make a list of points about cleanliness you need to stress to him or her – the need to wash cutlery properly, not just rinse it, for example, or the importance of putting rubbish out every week.

2 Now think of ways in which you can talk to the client about these topics in clear, suitable language that won't offend him or her. The next time you visit your client, raise the issues and try to arrive at a satisfactory conclusion.

Organising a space

You may well find that a client needs help to organise the room or rooms in which she lives so as to make the best use of space. This might involve helping someone to move into a single room to save heating costs, or to have everything close at hand if mobility is difficult.

Planning of this sort needs care and tact. Remember that it is the client's home, and that it is up to her to choose how it will look. Set against that are the needs of safety and hygiene. Do you have the right to persuade or force someone to get mobility aids or an orthopaedic mattress, or to throw out old papers and magazines because they are a fire risk? Discussion, sound good sense and compromise are often important here, with help and advice from your supervisor where you feel out of your depth.

If a special need arises, make sure the client knows where to go for help. This may involve you in contacting the social services department, a mobility officer or someone involved with needs assessment: your supervisor will give you the necessary addresses.

Once you're aware of the needs, and any special ways of satisfying them, help the client to organise her living space. This can often become an enjoyable session of discussion and planning, so make the most of this and encourage the client to talk freely and discuss several alternative approaches. Whatever you do, remember that it's not *your* home, and the client's rights are paramount.

ACTIVITY

1 With a client you visit regularly, draw a plan of the room or rooms he or she uses most often. Make paper cut-outs, to scale, of the pieces of furniture he or she has. Now move them around until you find a layout that your client likes, and that is attractive, safe and easy to maintain. Think carefully about how to reconcile these two demands – they may well conflict strongly.

2 When you've reached agreement – perhaps on a compromise – help your client rearrange the room accordingly.

With visually impaired clients you will need to use other approaches, perhaps getting the help of a specialist advisor from the care team – you will already have found out what help of this sort is available when you first got to know the client.

If you don't have a client in this position, try the exercise with a colleague playing the role of client.

Keeping safe

As far as practically possible, help the client to keep his home safe. This means practical things like making sure that carpets are not frayed, and that mats are not put over polished floors. It also means keeping rooms tidy, so that there are no piles of magazines where they can fall into fires, or trailing wires to trip over. Furniture needs to be in good repair, too, with no wobbly chairs, or tables with a short leg. Decoration matters, as well: not only does it make you feel better to live somewhere bright, but shabby surfaces trap dirt and germs. You can't, of course, force your own standards on people who wish to stay independent; but you can point out the advantages of keeping things tolerably clean.

If the client uses electrical or gas appliances, make sure that these are safe – simply rewiring a plug or replacing a frayed cord can prevent a potential fire and give great peace of mind. Be careful, though: if you repair something incorrectly, you may be legally responsible if an accident follows – check with your supervisor about your legal position. Try to make sure that appliances are used properly. This may need time and patience in explaining instructions, but it's a vital precaution.

The client's security needs thought, too. Someone living alone in an old house with no protection is easy prey to burglars and vandals. Advise your client to get help from a crime prevention officer, or if necessary get help yourself to see that she is safe from intruders.

You will also need to discuss ways of getting help in an emergency, through an emergency call or telephone link system. Your supervisor will have details of schemes and equipment that are available.

ACTIVITY

1 Visit a client you know and make a list of the hazards to both safety and security in his or her home. Sit down with the client and work out ways in which these can be eliminated.

2 With outside help if necessary, make changes so that your client is now safe and secure.

There is clearly a limit to how much responsibility you can take for the safety of clients who live in their own homes. You also have to respect their rights and their privacy. But careful and considerate advice, based on the relationship of trust you'll develop with your clients, will usually let you achieve a good deal in making a client's home clean, comfortable and safe – and how he wants it to be.

4.8 Managing at home

If you work with clients in their homes, you'll probably need to help them with routine matters – shopping, bills, form-filling, and making sure there are clothes to wear and sheets to sleep on. These may seem not to be important parts of the duties of a care worker, but they are vital for two reasons: they're basic to practical survival, and successfully carrying out domestic chores may be an immense and essential element of independence in your client's life. For you it's a chore; for him, it's therapy, and dignity as a human being living his own life. Don't forget that.

Clothes and bedclothes

Keeping clothes clean is one of the essential elements of running your own life, and the same is true of bedclothes. Do all you can to encourage your client to do his own laundry, especially if he isn't used to doing this – if he is recently bereaved, for example, or has just left hospital.

Discuss the ways in which this could be done: by visiting a launderette, perhaps, or by making sure the client knows how to use his own facilities. Make sure the area used for washing is kept clean, and that the equipment is safe – water and electricity are a lethal combination, so special care is needed here. If anything is wrong, report it or get it mended as soon as you can.

Using suitable language, talk about how often you need to do the washing. Talk, too, about the importance of washing soiled or infected linen and clothing as soon as possible, and the need to store freshly-washed and aired clothes where they'll stay clean.

Make sure that your client looks after clothing or sheets which are damaged – a session repairing a torn sheet, for example, can be a useful form of therapy as well as being of practical value. Encourage the client to get rid of clothing or bedclothes which are beyond repair; but remember the financial constraints that she may live under, or maybe just her habits of hoarding things.

How much you do yourself will depend largely on the client's need, but the aim here as so often is to get him to be self-sufficient. Encourage independence, but be ready to step in and help directly if necessary.

Shopping

Properly managed, a shopping expedition can be a source of pleasure and an enrichment of a client's sense of independence. As a result, encourage your client to shop alone as far as possible. Be aware, however, that a shopping trip with a friend or care worker can be very enjoyable for a lonely client.

Careful planning will not only help in practical arrangements but can also increase the pleasure. Talk over with your client:

- what it is that she needs;
- where it can be bought;
- whether she can afford it.

Then think carefully about transport. It's no use planning a trip on public transport if the client has difficulty walking; and someone who has claustrophobia won't be happy in a city-centre shopping mall.

When you're there, talk to the client about various goods that are available. Help her to make an informed choice within the practical and financial limits.

If you have to buy items for your client, make sure you follow her wishes as far as possible. Keep till receipts and any other documents and give them to the client with the change from any money she may have given you.

Explain what you've done, too – say how much the item was, why you bought it, and why you got that one rather than something similar from another shop. If there are any problems, make a clear record of them for your supervisor.

ACTIVITY

1 Talk to one of your clients about his or her shopping needs. Plan a shopping trip to buy an important item, following the procedure laid out above.

2 When you return, make sure that you sort out money properly. Think carefully about the trip, and make a few notes about what went well and what didn't go so well. Think about how you could improve it and make it more enjoyable next time.

Bills and forms

Some of your clients may need help with larger items of finance. Gas bills, electricity bills, rent – all of these have to be paid, and often there will be forms to be filled in, for example to claim Attendance Allowance or other benefits.

First of all, respect the client's privacy. If he can handle these things alone, that's fine: financial independence means a lot to many people, and being able to look after your affairs is a precious matter. If he does need help, though, you need to be methodical and accurate in your approach. Talk to him at every stage of the process, so that he knows exactly what's going on.

Check that the bill is accurate, and that it is for goods or services which have actually been received. Pay the account on time, in the way the client prefers – cash, cheque or whatever other system is practicable. Make sure you get a receipt, and give it to the client, making sure that he keeps it safely in case it's needed later.

ACTIVITY

1 Think about a client of yours. Make a list of the regular bills he or she has to pay. Next to each one, say how he or she pays it. Now think about any easier alternatives there might be – direct debits, savings stamps for a television licence, monthly payments for heating, for example.

2 Discuss these with your client to see whether you can make the business of paying bills easier.

ACTIVITY

Visit your local CAB. Collect as many leaflets as you can which are relevant to the kinds of financial problems your clients might have. Use these as a resource the next time a client has a problem with finances or with a service of some kind.

If any problems arise with money, you need to make a careful and complete note of their nature. If you're working with a care agency, get help from your supervisor. Sometimes you may need to complain or query a bill on a client's behalf; again, make sure that she knows what's going on and that, if necessary, you get professional help. Your local Citizens' Advice Bureau (CAB) or a specialist in the care team will give you advice.

The same is true of other matters relating to goods or services. If you need to help a client with a form – a census return, say, or an application for a grant or benefit – first talk it through carefully. Get the client to complete it as far as possible, but help as and when necessary.

You may also need to find out information about services or benefits, and tell the client. Whether you or your client contacts these support services will depend on the individual case. Whatever happens, make sure you know what's going on, and know where to go for professional help either yourself or for your client should you need to.

Heating

Making sure that clients keep warm is something of acute importance, particularly in severe winter weather. This is something which brings together many of the areas discussed here.

First, you'll need to make sure that your client has heating equipment which is effective and safe – check wires on electric heaters, and make sure that heating systems are serviced. Be especially careful with oil or liquid gas heaters: these may seem convenient, as they are relatively cheap and provide instant heat, but they are very dangerous in operation and cause condensation which leads to moulds and, consequently, to problems with health.

Make sure, too, that your client knows how to use a slot-meter for gas or electricity if there is one. Encourage him to keep a stock of suitable coins and to check the amount of credit remaining at regular intervals. Give advice about what to do in a power-cut – to keep a torch handy and have some alternative source of heat whenever possible.

If your client has worries about paying heating bills, talk about them and get advice. The CAB will help here, and the power companies themselves have various schemes. Remember that by law they are not allowed to disconnect power from elderly or disabled people. Here you can help by discussing problems with heating companies on behalf of your client, saving him from stress and embarrassment. If this is not something that falls within your job, make sure you refer the client to a social worker or community worker who can help.

ACTIVITY

1   Choose a client you visit regularly. Make a sheet of notes about his or her heating. Include details of:

(a) the kind of heating;
(b) the source of fuel (give the address, if necessary, for ordering new stocks).

2   Talk with your client to make sure he or she:

(a) knows what to do in case of power cuts;
(b) has made arrangements for paying for heating.

If there are problems with these, talk them over and try to solve them using the advice given above.

3   Now look at the client's heaters. Check that wires are not loose or frayed, and that there is no smell of gas or oil. If you're worried about anything, report it and get it repaired.

4   Whenever you visit your client, keep an eye open for problems of this sort and get them put right as soon as you can.

Appendix: organising your studies

This activity will make sure you get the most from using the book. Follow section A, B or C according to your own study circumstances.

A Informal training

If you're not working towards any qualification, you'll need to decide which parts you need to read and work through.

1 With the help of a supervisor or colleague, look at the contents list (pages iii and iv) to decide which sections are relevant to your needs.
2 Complete the Study Planner (see below) to give you a rough timetable.
3 On the Study Planner, make a note of any special help you might need – from specialist carers or a Citizens' Advice Bureau, for example.
4 Be prepared to revise or extend your Study Plan as your work and study develop. For example, you may find that some topics will take longer than you expected, or that some can be covered more quickly.

B NVQs/SVQs

1 Study the table of NVQ/SVQ units with the help of your supervisor or work assessor and decide which ones you are covering. He or she will have up-to-date details of all the units and their subsections or 'elements'. Note that the sections of the book referred to are only the main ones involved in each unit: you will have to use the Index to find other references to each topic.
2 Complete the Study Planner (below) to give you a rough timetable.
3 On the Study Planner, make a note of any special help you might need – from specialist carers or a Citizens' Advice Bureau, for example.
4 Discuss with your supervisor or work assessor the ways in which you can keep evidence of performance or knowledge to show the external assessor and to demonstrate your competence in each area. This might include:
   - keeping notes of discussions with clients;
   - keeping record cards of clients' needs for diet, hair care or personal hygiene;
   - making arrangements for your supervisor or a colleague to observe you carrying out a particular task over a period.
5 Be prepared to revise or extend your Study Plan as your work and study develop. For example, you may find that some topics will take longer than you expected, or that some can be covered more quickly.

C BTEC, City & Guilds or other qualification

1   With the help of your college tutor, look at the contents list (pages iii and iv) to decide which sections are relevant to your needs.

2   Complete the Study Planner (below) to fit in with the order in which the topics are covered in your course and work placement.

3   On the Study Planner, make a note of any special help you might need – from specialist carers or a Citizens' Advice Bureau, for example.

4   Discuss with your college tutor and work placement supervisor the ways in which you can keep evidence of performance or knowledge to satisfy the requirements of your course assessment. This might include:

- keeping notes of discussions with clients;
- keeping record cards of clients' needs for diet, hair care or personal hygiene;
- making arrangements for your supervisor or a colleague to observe you carrying out a particular task over a period.

5   Be prepared to revise or extend your Study Plan as your work and study develop. For example, you may find that some topics will take longer than you expected, or that some can be covered more quickly.

The NVQ/SVQ units

Level 2	Section of this book	Order of study	Facilities needed
Core			
Promote equality for all individuals	1.8, 2.1		
Contribute to the protection of individuals from abuse	1.7, 2.11		
Contribute to the ongoing support of clients and others significant to them	2.3		
Support clients in transition due to their care requirements	2.8		
Contribute to the health, safety and security of individuals and their environment	4.2		
Obtain, transmit and store information relating to the delivery of a care service	2.1		
Endorsements			
Developmental care			
Enable clients to move within their environment	2.8		
Enable clients to participate in recreation and leisure activities	2.9		
Contribute to the support of clients during development programmes and activities	2.9, 2.10		
Enable clients to maintain contact in potentially isolating situations	2.2, 2.3		
Maintain and control stock, equipment and materials	4.3		
Direct care			
Enable clients to exercise and use mobility appliances	3.6		
Contribute to the movement and treatment of clients to maximise their physical comfort	2.5		
Enable clients to maintain their personal hygiene and appearance	3.3		
Enable clients to eat and drink	3.7		
Enable clients to access and use toilet facilities	3.1		
Enable clients to achieve physical comfort	3.5		
Domiciliary support			
Contribute to the movement and treatment of clients to maximise their physical comfort	2.5, 2.10		
Enable clients to manage their domestic and personal resources	4.8		
Enable clients to maintain contacts in potentially isolating situations	2.2		
Contribute to the maintenance and management of domestic resources	4.6		
Residential/hospital support			
Contribute to the movement and treatment of clients to maximise their physical comfort	2.5		
Enable clients to eat and drink	3.7		
Enable clients to access and use toilet facilities	3.1		
Contribute to the maintenance and management of domestic resources	4.8		
Maintain and control stock, equipment and materials	4.3		
Special care needs			
Enable clients to maintain their personal hygiene and appearance	3.3		
Enable clients to eat and drink	3.7		
Enable clients to participate in recreation and leisure activities	2.9		
Enable clients to manage their domestic and personal resources	4.8		
Contribute to the support of clients during development programmes and activities	2.9, 2.10		
Enable clients to maintain contacts in potentially isolating situations	2.2, 2.3		

Study planner

Section title and number	Start date	Finish date	Sources of specialist help

Further reading

Age Concern. *Your Rights*. London: Age Concern. (Annual editions.)

Bond, M., and J. Kilty, 1986. *Practical Methods of Dealing with Stress*, 2nd edn. Guildford: University of Surrey.

Bookbinder, David 1987. *Housing Options for Older People*. London: Age Concern.

Butler, Keith, and Lynn Rayner 1991. *The New Handbook of Health and Preventive Medicine*. Loughton, Essex: Prometheus Books.

Department of Social Security. *What to do After a Death*. (Leaflet D49.)

Department of Transport. *A Guide to Transport for People with Disabilities*. (Annual editions.)

Eiser, Christine 1991. *Chronic Childhood Disease*. Cambridge: Cambridge University Press.

Feneley, R. C. L., and J. P. Blannin 1984. *Incontinence*. London: Churchill Livingstone.

Fleming, Ursula 1991. *Grasping the Nettle: a positive approach to pain*. London: Collins.

Good, Martin, and Andrew Pates (eds) 1989. *Second Chances: a national guide to adult education and training opportunities*: chapter 15, 'People with disabilities'. London: Department of Employment.

Gottesman, Meir (ed.) 1991. *Residential Child Care: an international reader*. London: Whiting & Birch.

Green, Jennifer 1991. *Death with Dignity*. London: Macmillan.

Hall, D. M. B., P. Hill and D. Elliman 1991. *The Child Surveillance Handbook*. Oxford: Radcliffe Medical Press.

Health Education Council 1986. *Who Cares? Information and support for the carers of confused people*. London: HEC (now Health Education Authority).

Henley, Alix 1979. *Asian Patients in Hospital and at Home*. London: King's Fund/Pitman Medical.

Henley, Alix 1983. *Caring for Hindus and their Families: religious aspects of care*. Cambridge: National Extension College.

Henley, Alix 1983. *Caring for Muslims and their Families: religious aspects of care*. Cambridge: National Extension College.

Henley, Alix 1983. *Caring for Sikhs and their Families: religious aspects of care*. Cambridge: National Extension College.

Hutchings, Sue, Jayne Comins and Judy Offiler 1991. *The Social Skills Handbook*. Bicester: Winslow Press.

Neuberger, Julia 1987. *Caring for Dying People of Different Faiths*. London: Austen Cornish.

Orton, Christine 1989. *Care for the Carer*. London: Thorsons.

Raphael-Leff, John 1991. *The Psychological Processes of Childbearing*. London: Chapman & Hall.

Sandford, Linda T. 1991. *Strong at the Broken Places: overcoming the trauma of childhood abuse*. London: Virago.

Sillars, Stuart 1991. *Success in Communication*, revised edn. 1988. London: John Murray.

Smyth, Terry 1992. *Caring for Older People: creative approaches to good practice*. Basingstoke: Macmillan.

Sonksen, P., C. Fox and S. Judd 1991. *Diabetes at Your Fingertips*. London: Class Publishing.

Squires, Amanda 1991. *Multicultural Health Care and Rehabilitation of Older People*. London: Edward Arnold and Age Concern.

Whittaker, Andrea 1991. *Service Evaluation by People with Learning Difficulties*. London: King's Fund.

Whittaker, Andrea 1991. *Supporting Self Advocacy*. London: King's Fund.

Young, Pat 1992. *Welfare Services: a guide for care workers*. Basingstoke: Macmillan.

Index